TEACHING CHILDREN TO LISTEN IN THE EARLY YEARS

TEACHING CHILDREN TO LISTEN IN THE EARLY YEARS

A PRACTICAL APPROACH

Liz Spooner and Jacqui Woodcock

FEATHERSTONE

LONDON OXFORD NEW YORK NEW DELHI SYDNEY

FEATHERSTONE
Bloomsbury Publishing Plc
50 Bedford Square, London, WC1B 3DP, UK

BLOOMSBURY, FEATHERSTONE and the Feather logo are trademarks of Bloomsbury Publishing Plc

First published in Great Britain, 2019 by Bloomsbury Publishing Plc

A catalogue record for this book is available from the British Library

ISBN: PB: 978-1-4729-5920-1

2 4 6 8 10 9 7 5 3 1

Typeset by Newgen KnowledgeWorks Pvt. Ltd., Chennai, India
Printed and bound in India by Replika Press Pvt. Ltd.

To find out more about our authors and books visit www.bloomsbury.com
and sign up for our newsletters

Contents

The appendices and illustrations for this book are available online at:
www.bloomsbury.com/Teaching-Children-To-Listen-Early-Years

Please type the URL into your web browser and follow the instructions to access the resources. If you experience any problems, please contact Bloomsbury at:
companionwebsite@bloomsbury.com

1

Why work on listening?

Listening underpins all language development and social interaction. Development of early listening skills in the first few months of life is necessary for children to successfully understand, use language and interact with those around them.

However, some children growing up in the twenty-first century may have early life experiences that make it challenging for them to develop the listening skills they need. Many young children find it hard to share attention with others, play independently, wait for their turn and follow an adult's lead. These difficulties become more apparent when children start attending educational settings, particularly when they have to share attention with a larger group of children. This impacts upon their ability to learn and make the educational progress that they are capable of. Poor listening also impacts on children's ability to make and maintain social relationships and play appropriately with others. Children who find listening challenging can be demanding of adult attention. Their behaviour can be distracting for other children or they might even interrupt others who are talking. When it goes wrong, listening can affect all aspects of the child's learning. Not only that, but the behaviours of that child can also adversely affect the listening environment for all children in Early Years settings.

Listening is a skill that children are genetically predisposed to learn. However, they need the appropriate opportunities and experiences to ensure they develop these skills securely. When children do not develop these skills naturally, they need to be explicitly taught them. It is possible to make significant differences to children's listening with a relatively small amount of explicit targeted intervention. *Teaching Children to Listen in the Early Years* is an evidence-based and practical approach that enables children to learn the listening skills they need. Better listening skills enable children to learn, play and make friends.

Developing an effective approach

We have all met children who find listening very difficult. However, in our own work, we have often found that the issue for many children was not that they were actually unable to listen, but rather that they did not understand what good listening was. With this observation in mind, we devised an approach to enable children to:

- learn the different behaviours they need to become good listeners
- understand how good listening can help them
- motivate them to show this behaviour independently.

This book will help you to teach children using this approach.

2
What is good listening?

Listening is not just one skill. Listening requires several skills which are brought together in order to focus successfully on another person.

There are four different behaviours that children need to learn in order to be a good listener:

* looking at the person who is talking
* staying quiet
* sitting still
* listening to ALL of the words.

Cue cards for all of these rules can be found in Illustration 1.

Looking at the person who is talking

This is a good rule to teach first. The games in this book support this because they use visual cues so that even children with significant language or learning difficulties or those with English as an additional language (EAL) can participate successfully.

It is important to establish that the rule is 'looking at the *person* who is talking' rather than 'good looking'. All children if asked would say they were good at looking but they need to know *who* they should be looking at in a particular situation. Some children may know that they need to look at the grown up at nursery or school but then do not generalise this skill to other people in different social contexts, e.g. when they are with their friends or their family.

The ability to look directly at the speaker is a good social rule to have for life. We want to teach children to be good listeners in every situation they will encounter. In order to do this, they need to learn that they have to look at the speaker and that this could be other children, different members of staff or members of their own family. Many of the play opportunities that children experience in Early Years settings will mean that children need to play alongside or cooperate with their peers. In order to do this successfully, they need to look at and respond to other children. Another reason to encourage children to look in the direction of the speaker is to help them read the non-verbal cues, such as gesture and facial expression, that we all use to support children's understanding.

The games in Chapter 5 are all designed so that eye contact gets an immediate and tangible reward. The games demonstrate to children that making eye contact with someone else enables them to find out extra information they would not have otherwise. This is very important if children are to understand the importance of eye contact and to generalise it as a skill in everyday life.

We have often been asked about the appropriateness and practicalities of using these games with children who are on the autistic spectrum. Almost every group of children we have worked with has included at least one child with a difficulty that falls somewhere on the autistic spectrum. Our experience has been that these children have fallen into two categories with regard to eye contact. The first group of children are not distressed in making eye contact but have not yet learned to use it naturally because they do not understand why it is helpful. This group of children respond really well to these games because the reward for eye contact is made much more explicit, which means they are far more motivated to use it. The second, and smaller group of children, actively dislike eye contact and find it uncomfortable. This group of children can still join in the games, but it may be helpful to modify expectations on their looking. For example, you could encourage them to look in the general direction of the person, perhaps focussing on their shoulder, rather than making direct eye contact. In our opinion, it is worth encouraging this, as looking at someone when they are talking is how we indicate interest in what the speaker is saying. Being able to use such a key social skill will help children to be more successful in making relationships with both their peers and with adults.

Staying quiet

When a group of children learns to stay silent, it has a huge impact on the listening environment for everyone. Children who talk at the same time as other people cannot process what they are hearing. Their talking also disrupts other children's listening, as well as distracting the adult who is leading the activity.

Early Years children can be impulsive and can find this rule challenging in a number of ways:

- Some children can shout out comments that are totally irrelevant to the lesson, e.g. 'I'm going on a plane in the holidays!'. These are impulsive children that need to tell you immediately when they have a thought in their head. Although this can be very disruptive, it is the easiest type of behaviour to manage because it is obvious that what they are saying is unconnected to the activity. Most adults feel comfortable in pointing this out and refocussing the child back on the topic or task at hand.

- A more challenging group are children who shout out answers or comments that *are* relevant to the topic but who do not put their hands up or wait to be chosen. These children are generally engaged and enthusiastic and they may not obviously present as having listening difficulties. These are challenging children to manage because, as an adult leading an activity, it is often quite encouraging to have a child who is engaged by the topic and wants to volunteer answers. However, when they shout out, they are disrupting the processing of other children who may have got to the answer if they had been given the time. In addition to this, learning to wait for your turn before speaking is an essential social skill required to be a successful communicator.

- Some children will talk to the children around them while the adult is speaking and not realise that this is not the expected behaviour. Most adults would feel uncomfortable talking at the same time as another person and would stop and wait for the other person to finish. However, many children, who have grown up with continual background noise, have become desensitised to talking over another person and need explicit teaching of this social rule.

Children who find it hard to stay quiet are often not aware that their behaviour can impact on their own and other children's listening. Consequently, the first step in teaching children to stay quiet is to raise their awareness of when they are talking at the same time as other people. They also need to have an opportunity to practise being quiet. The activities in Chapter 6 will give children the chance to experience being quiet and to see how this helps everyone to listen. However, it is equally important to be explicit about the behaviour required in order to get a turn, so try to make sure you only choose children when they are being quiet and not shouting out. It can be helpful to use phrases such as 'I am going to choose someone who remembered to put their hand up' or 'I can choose you now because you are being quiet'.

For all of these games, it is important to make links for children to other situations where staying quiet will help everyone to listen. If you can improve children's performance on this rule, it will make a huge impact on the listening and learning environment.

Sitting still

Children in the Early Years need to spend lots of time being active and playing both inside and outside. However, there are times when they need to listen during adult-led activities. Learning to sit still has a positive impact on their ability to stay focused during these times. Children who find it difficult to sit still can often distract themselves and other children around them.

Most children in the Early Years have single-channelled attention. This means that they can only focus on one thing at a time. Consequently, if they are distracted by something in their environment then they cannot focus on what the adult is saying.

When teaching children to sit still, it is helpful to build in an element which gives children feedback on their sitting and shows them when they are carrying out the rule successfully.

It can be helpful to practise these activities with children sitting on chairs before you try them with children sitting on the floor. Chairs are much easier for children to sit still on because they support children's core stability and organise their personal space. However, in the Early Years, children are often required to sit on the floor, so they need the opportunities to practise this rule in both situations. For children who find sitting on the floor difficult, it might be helpful for them to sit on a chair at times when they need to listen.

Do fidget toys help?

It is sometimes recommended that children have an object that they can fidget with unobtrusively. This can be helpful for some older children who are still struggling with sitting still. However, typically-developing children in Early Years have single-channelled attention. This means that if they are given an object to fidget with, it will be their sole focus. In order for a fidget toy to be a useful strategy, the child's attention levels need to have developed beyond this stage so that they are able to hold the toy and listen to what the adult is saying.

There are times when a fidget toy can be helpful to manage the behaviour of highly-distractable children. It does not help them to listen but can occupy them at times when their behaviour might distract other children, e.g. during story time or assembly. If a toy is used for this purpose, then it is important to remember to take the distraction away when you need them to focus again.

Listening to all of the words

There are several different reasons why children don't listen to all of the words in an instruction:

- Some children have not learned that 'everyone' means them too. These children need instructions to be directed specifically to them because they are unlikely to follow instructions that are given to the whole class. They may only listen if their name is called.

- Other children may listen to the first part of an instruction, recognise the scenario, think they know what is coming next, and then stop listening. Children who do this can often have good understanding of language, but they are caught out when the instruction is different from the one they predicted.

- With a familiar activity, children may not listen at all as they have already experienced the task and think they know the routine. As Early Years settings are often quite predictable environments, this can occur frequently. Of course, the problems then occur when they are being asked to do something new or different.

- An instruction may contain a 'trigger phrase' such as, 'line up at the door' or 'it's nearly snack time'. When children hear a phrase like this, it is often the end of any attempt at listening and they do not pay attention to anything else in the instruction, but they do carry out this part of the instruction.

- Educational practitioners are often very 'fair' and ensure that everyone has a turn to speak or to do an activity. However, many children will switch off once they have had a turn because they know they won't get chosen again, so they think they don't need to listen any more.

The games to teach this rule in Chapter 8 put children in situations where they have to listen to *all* of the words in order to successfully carry out the activity. The first games to teach this rule involve listening to musical instruments or just single words to make them more accessible to all Early Years children, including those with English as an additional language and those with special educational needs.

3

Identification, target setting and evaluating outcomes

We can recognise when children are not demonstrating good listening skills, but it can be more difficult to identify exactly what it is that they are doing wrong. The listening skills rating scale (Appendix 1) is quick to use and allows you to rate children on each of the four rules of good listening discussed in the previous chapter.

	Score	1	2	3	4
Looking at the person who is talking		Does not initiate eye contact simultaneously.	Some eye contact but not sustained.	Initiates eye contact but needs recall.	Appropriate eye contact when listening.
Staying quiet		Consistently interrupts/talks when adult is talking.	Occasionally quiet but cannot maintain this.	Some talking but can be recalled to stay quiet and listen.	Quiet when listening as part of a group.
Keeping still		Not able to stay on floor/mat. Constantly fidgets.	Inappropriate sitting posture/lots of fidgeting.	Stays on floor/mat but some fidgeting.	Appropriate balanced sitting.
Listening to all of the words		Does not respond to name. Does not respond to simple instructions.	Relies mostly on routine/copies others. Needs repeated reminders.	Follows very short instructions but needs repetition of more complex information.	Able to follow two-step instructions.
Total listening score					

Table 1. Listening rating scale. This is available for you to photocopy and use in Appendix 1.

By using the rating scale, you can obtain an individual score for each of the four components of listening, as well as a total score. In the work we have done with children, we have classified scores in the following way:

A score of below 8: Severe listening difficulties
A score of between 8 and 11: Moderate listening difficulties
A score of 12 and above: Adequate listening skills

The rating scale enables children's listening to be objectively measured and allows teaching staff to focus intervention on the specific areas of listening that most need development. Some children have difficulties in all four areas of listening, whereas others may only have difficulties with one or two rules. During our work with children, we often see two types of poor listeners. These are explained in detail below.

1. The active poor listener

These children are easy to spot. They are often enthusiastic and engaged by an adult-led activity. This means they show good abilities in 'looking at the person who is talking' and 'listening to all of the words'. However, they tend to score more poorly on 'staying quiet' and 'sitting still'. Their impulsive behaviour means they can distract themselves and other children around them. They find it difficult to stay quiet but may be listening to what the adult says and will shout out information relevant to the activity. The problem is that when they are talking, they disrupt the processing of other children who are trying to listen. Waiting for your turn to speak is an important social skill for any group activity that will help children to form positive relationships with their peers.

2. The passive poor listener

These children are less noticeable within a group. They are usually quiet and can sit still during a group activity. They may not always look at the person who is talking. If you are working with a large group of children, you may not notice a child that transgresses this rule. These children also score particularly poorly on 'listening to all of the words'. This often only becomes apparent when children have to carry out tasks after listening to an explanation from the adult as, because they have not listened, they do not know what to do.

Appendix 2 is a group intervention evaluation form to photocopy. This will enable you to use the rating scale to establish a baseline before intervention. You can then rate children again to provide a measure of the outcomes that you have achieved.

Setting SMART targets

Specific

Setting targets for a specific rule that a child finds challenging helps to develop their insight into the behaviour they need to change. With children who have difficulties in all areas, choosing one rule to focus on increases their chance of achieving change quickly.

It is also helpful to be specific about the context in which you are aiming to see the behaviour. Examples of a specific target might be:

- 'Amelia to stay quiet when other children answer the register'
- 'Malachi to sit still while we hand out the whiteboards and pens'
- 'Hassan to look at his learning partner when talking on the mat'
- 'Lucy to listen to all the words at choosing time'.

Measurable

Use the listening rating scale to rate children's skills at the time the target is set and again at the time of review to measure their progress. An example of a measurable target might be:

- 'Alex to achieve a level 3 for looking at the person who is talking during show and tell (currently level 1)'.

Attainable

Different environments create different challenges for children's listening. It is usually easiest for children to keep listening when working one-to-one before moving on to sharing attention in paired work with another child. Small group work is usually more difficult and listening as part of a larger group is the biggest challenge. It can be helpful to set targets for less challenging environments and allow the child to experience some success before moving on to situations where they must share attention with many other children.

Similarly, it is unrealistic to expect children to carry out their target for a whole session. Setting a target for a small amount of time, such as five minutes, will allow a child to achieve some success. You can then extend the amount of time that you are expecting them to carry out the behaviour. Examples of attainable targets might be:

- 'Ellie-May to stay quiet while another child has a turn in a paired activity'
- 'Ollie to look at the teacher when she calls his name at snack time'.

Relevant

The obstacles which cause children to have difficulties with listening can be varied. This means that two children can both have significant difficulties with listening but these difficulties might be presented very differently. It is therefore important to match the target to the area which will have the greatest impact for each child, as you can see in these quick case studies.

Connor, aged four

Connor is a chatty and enthusiastic boy who finds it hard to wait for his turn and stay quiet. (Looking:3/Staying quiet:1/Keeping Still: 2/Listening to all of the words:2 = Active poor listener.)

A relevant target might be 'Connor to stay quiet during one page of a story at circle time'.

Demi, aged three

Demi is a quiet girl who needs encouragement to join in activities and rarely initiates communication. (Looking:1/Staying quiet:4/Sitting still:3/Listening to all of the words:1 = Passive poor listener.)

A relevant target might be 'Demi to look at the adult when her name is called'.

Time Framed

With explicit teaching, children can make progress quickly with their listening. The results from our own work, which are displayed in Chapter 12, were achieved in six weeks with once-a-week intervention and embedded strategies. Providing realistic targets have been set, change can be achieved in this time scale. An example of a time framed target might be:

- 'Taylor to reach level 3 for staying quiet in small group activities by the end of spring term'.

Helping children to generalise skills

Transferring skills across contexts

Children can often learn skills in a very rigid and specific way. For example, they can sometimes show good listening in a familiar activity with their key worker but then do not show the same behaviour when a new member of staff takes the group. It can be helpful to set explicit targets with them to help them transfer their skills to other contexts, e.g. 'Hannah to look at Mrs Smith in forest school when we sit in the circle'.

Anticipating challenges to listening

Children's listening can sometimes be affected by factors that adults can recognise but that the children themselves are unaware of. Staff know the children they work with well and often anticipate who will find an activity challenging and what might go wrong. Intervening *before* this happens and setting it as a challenge that has to be overcome helps children to develop insight and gives them the opportunity to develop some control over their own behaviour. This helps to build children's self-esteem. Conversely, waiting until after the event means that staff have to manage the behaviour rather than the child having the chance to do so. For example, you could say, 'Codie – I am a bit worried that if I choose someone else to have the first turn you will be grumpy and make a noise. Do you think you can stay quiet even if I choose Samir to go first?'. Most children, if the challenge is set up this way, will try very hard to comply and then you can praise them for their positive choice.

Helping children to develop insight

Staff are always able to identify children who are not a good combination when they play or sit together. Unfortunately, when given the choice these children always want to be together. There are two ways of dealing with this. Firstly, you can manage the behaviour each time it occurs by deciding where children should sit for them. This is a valid approach, but it is likely that you will need to use the same approach every day. Alternatively, you can help the children to develop some insight into their behaviour by being explicit about your concerns, e.g. 'Noah and Mackenzie – I am a bit worried that if you sit together on the carpet you will talk to each other. If you sit together today can you sit still, stay quiet and look at me?'. Then, at the end of the activity, you can talk to the children about how well they did. If they weren't able to achieve their target, explain this and sit them separately again next time. You can then revisit the challenge later to give them another opportunity to show good listening despite the challenge.

4

How to use the activities

Who can you use the activities with?

The games are designed to be used with children from about three to five years old. However, they can also be used with older children who are working at this developmental level. Ideas for babies and toddlers are included in Chapter 9. The games within each section are organised in a hierarchy and start with activities which are most accessible for younger children. However, within each game we have included ways to make them easier or harder so that you can differentiate depending on the needs of your group.

Groups

Setting up the room

When starting a group, we would recommend children sitting on chairs for the first few sessions, if possible, as this will support their listening. Whether on chairs or sitting on the floor, children need to be in a circle. Adults need to be sitting in the circle with the children as part of the group.

How many children should I have in my group?

Younger children in Early Years find it very hard to share attention. We would recommend that, for this age, the activities should be delivered in smaller groups. The following is a guideline to group size according to the age range of the children you are working with:

Three-year-olds	Small groups of four-to-six children
Four-year-olds	Groups of six-to-eight children
Reception	Whole class

Table 2. Guidelines for group sizes.

These are guidelines only and staff can choose to be flexible according to the needs of their group. However, it is important to ensure that the groups are large enough so that children can experience sharing adult attention and waiting for their turn. This will help them to generalise the skills required for the game to other group contexts.

Once children have started school, we would recommend the approach being used with whole classes. Our experience has shown us that if the whole class learn rules together it gives them a shared understanding and consistent set of expectations. This effect is difficult to achieve if a small group is taken out of the class to work on listening.

Staffing the groups

We would recommend that, whenever possible, large groups and whole class work are delivered by two adults. Two adults working together enables:

- one adult to introduce an activity and another to model the target behaviour
- one adult to monitor and manage any behaviour issues, freeing the other adult to focus on leading the activity
- the supporting adult to encourage children to comply with the target behaviour using non-verbal prompts such as gesture or sign.

Ideally, one of the adults leading the group should be someone who works with the children at other times. This may be their class teacher or key worker. This allows them to remind the children that staff know the behaviour that they are capable of and encourages children to carry over their good listening to other situations. It also ensures that children will know that the expectations of their listening will be high and consistent throughout the day.

What should I do if children do not comply?

You will encounter several types of non-compliance:

Children who cannot yet follow an adult's lead

In order to access any group activity, a child needs to be able to comply with an adult-led activity for a short period of time. If they are not yet ready to do this, then we would recommend spending time to help the child to share attention with you, focussing together on the same activity. Appendix 4 has some ideas for working on shared attention with a child who needs this level of intervention first before working with other children in a group.

Children who want to comply but find listening challenging

It is inevitable when running a group to improve listening that you will have children in your group who find listening a challenge! These children often want to please you but have very little awareness of their behaviour and the impact it can have on their listening. The best way to manage this kind of child is to be explicit about what they are doing and what the target behaviour is, e.g. 'Zak I really want to choose you for this game, but I can't because you are shouting out at me. I'm going to really watch you next time to see if you can stay quiet.' Then, carefully watch for the child to briefly show the target behaviour (this may be only a few seconds) and praise them straightaway, e.g. 'Zak I'm so proud of you! I can choose you now – you stayed really quiet!'. This is a very positive and effective way of helping these children to develop their insight and gain more control over their own behaviour.

Children who deliberately disrupt

Children who deliberately disrupt are much less common, particularly in Early Years, but are much more challenging to deal with. As the approach is based on games, children's motivation to comply and be included is usually high. However, it is impossible to run the games successfully with a child being disruptive, so this kind of behaviour must be managed before the game continues. Here are some approaches you could try:

- If you know the children you are working with well, you may be able to anticipate non-compliant or disruptive behaviour before it occurs. In this case, you can set the children a challenge, e.g. 'Kieran, I want to choose you for this game, but I'm worried that you might be a bit silly and try to make the other children laugh. If I choose you, can you do your best sitting?'. It is then really important to praise the child when they meet your challenge. In our experience, the vast majority of children want to please adults and, when given a specific target, they will rise to the challenge.

- You will not be able to predict all the behavioural incidents that might occur. If you are faced with a child who is not following the rules then challenge this immediately, e.g. 'Taylor, I'm sad because you pointed and spoiled the game. I need you to keep your hands still. Can you do that?'. Then continue with the game. If they persist in being non-compliant then you will need the other adult to remove them from the game until they are ready to comply.

- In our experience, children who are removed from a group activity usually want to return and join in but don't understand they need to comply with the same rules as the other children. You can support them by giving them clear explicit guidance about the behaviour everyone else is showing that they will also need to show, e.g. 'Jayden, do you want a turn at this game? I need you to stay on your chair the same as everyone else. Can you do that?'.

How do I make sure the games work?

Although the games might appear simple, the children you will use them with are not! Our tips for success are:

Be a role model

Always introduce each game by modelling the activity with an adult first so that the children know what the target behaviour is. This technique of showing as well as telling is good practice for all children, not just those with listening and language problems.

Establish the ground rules

However easy the games seem, take the time to read the 'ground rules' and 'inside information' before you start. We have played these games many times and these sections should help you to learn from our mistakes and get the most out of the games. Always take the time to establish the ground rules with the children before you start, e.g. 'There are two rules for this game. One, everyone has to stay quiet. Two, everyone looks at the person with the blindfold'. Then make sure everyone is complying with the rules before continuing with the game.

Differentiating activities

Planning the game at the right level can make the difference between success and failure. Use the 'make it harder/make it easier' suggestions to start the activity at the right level. If in doubt, start at the easier level and work up. If an activity seems to be too challenging, then do not be afraid to swap to an easier version mid-game. It is better to do this than to keep going with an activity that is not working.

Use the power of motivation

If you make a game harder without telling the children that is what you are doing, then you miss out on an opportunity. Saying, 'We're going to do it again but make it more difficult' creates a challenge and increases both children's motivation and their self-esteem.

Don't be predictable

Avoid choosing children to have a turn in a predictable order. Always choosing children in a predictable sequence can encourage children to switch off once they have had a turn. Instead, say 'I am looking to see who I can choose'. Then, when you choose someone tell the group why that person is getting a turn, e.g. 'I could choose you because you were looking at me'. This approach will mean that some children will have more turns than others, but it also means that all children are more likely to sustain their focus and comply in order to get chosen.

What format do you recommend for a group?

The activities are designed to run as a weekly intervention. How long each session lasts will depend on the age group you are working with:

Three-year-olds	**20 – 25 minutes**
Four-year-olds	**25 – 30 minutes**
Reception	**35 – 45 minutes**

Table 3. Recommended session lengths.

Frequent changes of activities and the opportunity to move around enables most children to sustain their focus for this length of time. Using the same 'hello' and 'goodbye' song each week when delivering these sessions to a small group helps to give a clear signal for the start and end and gives children an opportunity to participate socially. It also gives all the children the chance to hear and learn the names of the other children in the group. (See Appendix 3 for hello and goodbye songs.)

Typical format for group work

All children are helped by structure and routine. Having a familiar format for each group will help children to feel more confident about participating even when the activities change. A typical format is shown below:

- 'Hello' song or similar
- Four games – one for each of the four rules
- Identify a challenge for the week, e.g. 'We are going to remember our keeping still at story time'
- 'Goodbye' song.

A sample 6-week plan for small group work can be found in Appendix 4.

Typical format for whole-class work

It is more challenging for children to listen when they are part of a much larger group. A familiar structure enables children to understand the expectations on their listening behaviour and frequent changes in activities help them to keep focussed.

- Introduction or reinforcement of the four rules
- Four games – one for each of the four rules
- A final activity which reinforces all of the rules
- Summary of the rules
- Identify a class listening challenge for the week, e.g. 'We are going to remember to sit still when we are holding our whiteboards and pens'.

A sample 6-week plan for whole-class work (recommended for children four years and above) can be found in Appendix 5.

What equipment do I need?

The games generally use equipment that would be available in a typical Early Years setting. There are also a range of useful game resources available as Appendices. If you are planning on running regular listening intervention within your setting, then it will be useful to assemble all the equipment you need into a listening box. This will make it much easier for you to deliver the intervention with minimum preparation before each session. Suggested equipment for your listening box is listed below.

Listening box equipment

- Photocopiable resources from this book
- Variety of 'Who looks different props' obvious (e.g. Policeman's hat) and subtle (e.g. real glasses)
- Mats
- Picnic blanket
- Blindfold
- Timer
- Bubbles
- Bag of musical instruments
- Sound toy
- Stacking boxes
- Selection of noise makers, e.g. hot potato toy
- Bunch of keys and box
- Pop up tunnel
- Pass the turn games appropriate to age, e.g. Pop up pirate, Marble run, or a car ramp and toy cars.

General ground rules when carrying out activities

All of the games have specified ground rules, but these are the general rules that we work to:

- Not everyone has a turn during activities.
- Establish the behaviour needed in order to get a turn at the beginning of each game.
- Be explicit to specific children in the group about why they are not getting chosen and explain what they need to do, e.g. 'Charlie, I really want to choose you to have a turn, but can I choose you when you are talking? I'm going to be watching you and when you are quiet I will be able to give you a turn'.
- During the session, give specific praise to children for good listening behaviour, e.g. 'Boys, I can see you are ready to listen because you are looking at me. You're showing everyone what to do'.

Framework for all game instructions

All the games are laid out in the following format:

Rule

Game number

Name of the game	
How to play	**Description of the game.**
Equipment	**What you need to play.**
Ground rules	**Basic rules that need to be established before you start to make sure children understand the target behaviour.**
Inside information	**Extra information that we have learned from playing the games lots of times with lots of children, which will help you carry them out successfully.**
Differentiation	**Suggestions for adapting the games to make them easier or harder for different ages and abilities or to enable progression.**

5

Games: Looking at the person who is talking

Looking at the person who is talking

Game 1

'The Looking Song'

How to play

The children sit in a circle. Sing the 'Looking Song' (to the tune of 'Wind the Bobbin Up') and encourage the children to join in the actions.

> Blink your eyes at me. Blink your eyes at me. Blink. Blink. Blink. Blink. Blink
> Wink your eyes at me. Wink your eyes at me. Wink. Wink. Wink. Wink. Wink.
> Look at the ceiling. Look at the floor.
> Look at the window. Look at the door.
> Shut your eyes tightly one, two, three.
> Open your eyes and look at me.

Equipment

- None

Ground rules

- Wait for everyone to look at you before starting the song.

Inside information

- Model the actions you want the children to carry out.

- This is a useful activity to include at the start of any circle time to encourage the children to focus on you before the session begins.

Differentiation

Easier

- Point as well as look to the places around the room.

Harder

- Go very slowly on the counting so the children have to wait longer before opening their eyes to look at you.

Looking at the person who is talking

Game 2

Who's got the glasses?

How to play

With small groups, show the children the glasses and allow each child to try them on. Then, choose one child to wear the blindfold and another to wear the glasses. Once all of the children are following the ground rules, the child can take the blindfold off. They can then look around the group and point to who is wearing the glasses.

Equipment

- Selection of glasses
- Blindfold

Ground rules

- Everyone has to stay quiet.
- Everyone has to look at the person with the blindfold.
- Everyone has to keep their hands still.

Inside information

- Choose a child who is happy to wear the blindfold first. If other children are uncomfortable wearing a blindfold, then an adult can help them hide their eyes.
- Start with using the same glasses for each turn so that children know what to look for. Then, try using different glasses for each turn.

Differentiation

Easier

- An adult leads the child round the circle to encourage them to look at each child.

Harder

- In a small group, you can try giving all but one child glasses to wear and asking the child with the blindfold to find someone who is not wearing glasses.

Looking at the person who is talking

Game 3

Round and round the hat goes

How to play

One child is chosen to sit on a chair in the middle of the circle and wear a blindfold. The other children pass round a hat while everyone says the rhyme 'round and round the hat goes, where it stops, nobody knows'. When the rhyme stops, the person holding the hat puts it on. Once the ground rules are established, the child with the blindfold takes it off and looks around the circle to find the person with the hat.

Equipment

- Hat
- Blindfold

Ground rules

- Everyone has to pass the hat on.
- Everyone has to look at the person with the blindfold.
- Everyone has to keep their hands still.

Inside information

- The adults might need to help the children pass the hat on.
- An adult must ensure that the child with the blindfold waits until the group is ready for them to look.

Differentiation

Easier

- An adult leads the child round the circle to encourage them to look at each child.

Harder

- The adults can wear the hat too.
- Use different hats each time.
- Have two hats going around the circle so the child has to find two people.

Looking at the person who is talking

Game 4

Find the space

How to play

One child is chosen to sit in the middle of the circle and wear a blindfold. This will leave an empty chair in the circle. Another child is then chosen to change places and sit on the empty chair. The first child then takes the blindfold off and has to find the new empty chair to sit on.

Equipment

- Blindfold

Ground rules

- Everyone has to look at the person in the middle of the circle.

- Everyone has to stay quiet.

- The child who is chosen to move has to walk quietly to their new chair.

Inside information

- An adult must ensure that the child with the blindfold waits until the second child has moved.

- This is a useful game to help children to organise where they sit and find a space quickly.

Differentiation

Easier

- Let the child get up and walk round the edge of the circle to find the space.

Harder

- Rearrange the whole group while the child is wearing a blindfold by asking everyone to move to a different space in the circle.

- Use a 30-second sand timer so they have to find the space before the sand runs out.

Looking at the person who is talking

Game 5

Where's the bear?

How to play

The children sit in a circle. Three boxes are placed in the centre of the circle. One child is chosen to go out of the room. A teddy is hidden under one of the boxes. The rest of the children have to stay quiet and look at the box where the teddy is hiding.

The first child comes back in and has to work out where the bear is by looking at the direction of the other children's eye contact.

Equipment

- Three boxes
- A teddy bear

Ground rules

- Everyone has to stay quiet.
- Everyone has to sit still.
- Everyone else must keep looking at the box when the child comes back in.

Inside information

- Many young children will be impulsive and want to point to the box. You will need to be explicit about sitting still, staying quiet and just using their eyes to show where teddy is.

Differentiation

Easier

- Only use two boxes.

Harder

- Move the boxes closer together.
- Choose just one person to look at the box to show where teddy is. The other children should look at the child who went out of the room.

Looking at the person who is talking

Game 6

Who is hiding?

How to play

One child puts on a blindfold. Another child in the group is chosen to go out of the room. The first child takes off the blindfold and looks carefully at the group and decides who is missing.

Equipment

- Blindfold

Ground rules

- The child who is chosen to go out has to do so quietly and cannot speak.

- Everyone has to keep looking at the person with the blindfold.

Inside information

- Only do this game with a group of children who are familiar with each other.

- Encourage the child to look at the group before they put on the blindfold.

Differentiation

Easier

- Leave the empty chair in the circle while the child is out of the room.

Harder

- Take the child's chair away once they leave the room.

- Get all the other children in the group to change places.

Looking at the person who is talking

Game 7

Who's cross?

How to play

Show the children the happy and cross cue cards and practise making these faces. One child then puts on a blindfold. Another child in the group is given the cross cue card. They have to sit on the card to hide it. Then, they must make the cross face. Everyone else has to make a happy face. The first child has to take off the blindfold and look at all the children's faces to find out who is cross.

Equipment

- Emotion cue cards (Illustration 2)
- Blindfold

Ground rules

- Everyone has to keep looking at the person with the blindfold.
- Everyone apart from the child with the cross card has to make a happy face.

Inside information

- Spend time practising making the faces and choose a child that you know can make the face and sustain it for a while.
- Don't let the child take the blindfold off until everyone else is making a happy face.
- Lead the child around the group and encourage them to look at each face.
- Children sometimes want to make accompanying noises, e.g. growling while making a cross face. You need to be explicit that they must only use their face to show that they are cross.

Looking at the person who is talking

Game 8

Make the face

How to play

The children sit in a circle. Put the emotion cue cards in a bag. Pass the bag around from child to child and say the rhyme 'Round and round the faces bag goes. Where it stops nobody knows'. When the rhyme finishes, the child holding the bag takes out a cue card and makes the same face. The other children have to look carefully and guess which cue card they have got.

Equipment

- Emotion cue cards (Illustration 2)
- Bag

Ground rules

- The child has to choose the cue card but keep it hidden while they make the face. You will need to model this first.
- The cue cards go back in the bag for the next turn.

Inside information

- Start the bag at a different point in the circle each time.
- Practise all the faces before you start the game.

Differentiation

Easier

- Only put happy and cross faces into the bag.

Harder

- Choose only one child to guess the face.
- Use all four cue cards.

Looking at the person who is talking

Game 9

Who is next?

How to play

Select a motivating activity or game which is appropriate to the age of the group. This could be building a tower with bricks, a car ramp or marble run or taking a turn in a commercial game. Explain that you are going to give lots of people a turn, but you are NOT going to say their name. You are going to look at them and give them a little nod to let them know whose turn is next.

Equipment

- Age-appropriate game or activity

Ground rules

- If you want a turn you must look at the leader.

- The leader ONLY chooses people who are looking at them, sitting still and staying quiet.

- If you carry on demonstrating good looking you might get another turn.

Inside information

- You can play this game without an activity as long as the reward for looking is something motivating, e.g. lining up at the door before going out to play. This is a really good way to move children from one activity to another in a silent and orderly manner.

- This is a good game to practise lots of listening skills, such as looking, staying quiet and sitting still. It can be played lots of times without the children losing motivation, as long as the activity is changed regularly.

- Make sure you set the ground rules in advance, e.g. 'If you want a turn, who do you need to look at? Am I going to choose anyone who is shouting out?'

- Look out for someone who is still doing good looking even after they have had a go and give them another turn as soon as possible. This will stop children from switching off when they have had a turn and motivate them to keep looking.

Differentiation

Easier

- Make it easier by nodding and then also waving at the child who has the next turn.

Harder

- Choose a child to be the 'teacher' and to give the turns by nodding at the other children. Make sure they understand that they need to choose children who are looking at them and staying quiet.

Looking at the person who is talking

Game 10

Who's got the crown?

How to play

The children sit in a circle. Show the children the crown cue card and tell them that someone is going to be chosen to be the king or queen and they will hide the crown cue card. Then, send one child out of the room. A second child is given the crown and sits on it to hide it. All the other children have to look at the king or queen but they cannot talk. The first child comes back in and has to guess who has the crown by looking at the direction of the other children's gaze.

Equipment

- Crown cue card (Illustration 12)

Ground rules

- Everyone has to keep looking at the person with the crown.

- Everyone has to keep their hands still.

- Everyone has to stay quiet and just use their eyes to show where the crown is.

Inside information

- This is a useful game for children to learn how to read eye gaze in order to work out where to focus.

- Many young children will be impulsive and want to point to the person. You will need to be explicit about sitting still, staying quiet and just using their eyes to show where the king or queen is.

Differentiation

Easier

- The child has three guesses to find out who has the crown.

Harder

- Only the children (not the adult) look at the king or queen.

6

Games: Staying quiet

Staying quiet

Game 1

Sound boxes

How to play

One child puts on a blindfold or goes out of the room. A musical toy or music player is hidden under one of the boxes. The child then takes off the blindfold and then has to listen to find which box the noise is coming from.

Explain the game to the children and then ask the group 'What can we do to help them do really good listening?'. Hopefully, someone in the group will suggest being quiet. When they do, you need to reinforce this, e.g. 'What a good idea! If we are really quiet, then that will help them to do really good listening. If we are noisy they won't be able to hear that little noise.' Then, play the game.

Equipment

- Musical toy or phone playing music
- Three boxes
- Blindfold (if needed)

Ground rules

- Everyone has to stay quiet.
- Everyone has to look at the person with the blindfold.
- You must listen to all the boxes first and then you decide which one to turn over.

Inside information

- You MUST get an adult to model this activity first. Children always want to solve these tasks visually and will just lift up boxes to look underneath, unless an adult models how to get down and listening with their ear on the box first.
- In addition to practising keeping quiet, this game is also a sound localisation game. This is an important skill for the educational setting and conversation generally, so that children can hear a voice and know where to look.

Differentiation
Easier

- Use a really noisy toy or phone with the volume turned up.
- Only use two boxes.
- Put the boxes far apart.

Harder

- Use a very quiet toy or turn the volume down.
- Put the boxes close together.

Staying quiet

Game 2

Hunt the sound

How to play

One child goes out of the room. A musical toy or phone is hidden somewhere in the room. The child then comes back into the room and then has to listen and find the sound.

First, explain the game to the children and then ask the group 'What can we do to help them do really good listening?'. Hopefully, someone in the group will suggest being quiet. When they do you need to reinforce this, e.g. 'What a good idea! If we are really quiet, then that will help them to do their best listening. If we are noisy they won't be able to hear the noise.' Then play the game.

Equipment

- Musical toy or phone playing music

Ground rules

- Everyone has to stay quiet.

- Everyone has to look at the person trying to find the toy.

- When you come back into the room, stand still and listen first, before trying to find the sound.

Inside information

- Again, children will want to solve this task visually and will tend to race around the room at top speed looking for the noise maker. You must model standing in the middle of the room and listening first.

- You must establish the ground rule 'Everyone has to look at the person trying to find the toy' or children will look at the hidden noise maker and give the game away. If you know you have children within the group who will find it hard not to look at the toy, then give them this as a challenge, e.g. 'Do you know, I really want to put this toy behind your chair but I'm a bit worried that you will turn around and look at it and spoil the game. Can I trust you to be really sensible and just look at the person with the blindfold?' Then give them lots of praise when they do this. In our experience, children will always rise to the challenge.

- Look out for other noise-making items that you can hide, e.g. toys that talk; toys that make intermittent noises, etc.

Differentiation

Easier

- Use a really noisy toy or a phone with the volume turned up.

Harder

- Use a very quiet toy or a phone on low volume.

- Hide a toy which makes a funny noise. This will make the children want to laugh so they will need to exert self-control to stay quiet. This is what we want children to do when listening in a group.

Staying quiet

Game 3

Putting toys to bed

How to play

Explain to the group that it is time for the toys to go to bed and we need to be really quiet to help them sleep. Then, choose one child to put a toy in the bed. The group then sings 'Night night teddy, night night teddy, night night teddy, it's time to go to sleep'. The adult turns the day/night cue card to night and then counts using fingers to five while everyone stays quiet. The adult then turns the sign to daytime and the child can wake teddy up by playing the musical instrument.

Equipment

- Choice of character toys (children can say the toy's name instead of teddy if they want)
- Toy bed and blankets
- Night-time and daytime cue cards (Illustration 3)
- Musical instrument

Ground rules

- Everyone has to stay quiet while the toys are sleeping.
- The child can only play the instrument when the adult turns the sign to daytime.

Inside information

- This is a good game for impulsive children as it teaches them to wait for an adult signal before carrying out an activity.
- Using your fingers while quietly counting as the toys are asleep will help focus the attention of the children in the group.

Differentiation

Easier

- Have the instrument by the adult so the child has to stand up and get it when the sign turns to daytime.

Harder

- The child has to hold the instrument still and stay quiet while the toy is sleeping.
- Increase the number you count to, before turning the daytime sign round.

Staying quiet

Game 4

Stop/go musical instruments

How to play

Each child is given an instrument to play with briefly and then puts it on the floor in front of them. They have to watch the adult's sign and, when it is turned to 'go', they can play their instruments until it turns to 'stop'. They then have to put their instruments back on the floor until the sign is turned to 'go' again.

Equipment

- Musical instruments

- Stop and go signs (Illustration 4)

Ground rules

- The adult chooses an instrument for each child.

- Everyone has to put their instrument on the floor.

- Everyone has to look at the adult with the stop/go sign.

Inside information

- It helps to focus children if you count out loud before turning the sign around, e.g. 'We got to three last time. How long can we stay quiet this time? One… two… three… four'.

- Begin by only turning the sign to 'stop' for a short amount of time.

Differentiation

Easier

- Only wait a second or two before turning the sign round.

Harder

- Increase the amount of time the children have to wait before playing.

- The children have to hold their instrument, but stay quiet, when the sign is turned to 'stop'.

Staying quiet

Game 5

'Dinosaur Stamp' song

How to play

Sing and act out the 'Dinosaur Stamp' song (to the tune of 'Row, Row, Row Your Boat'). Encourage the children to make the dinosaur verse very loud and the mouse verse very quiet. Hold up the appropriate dino-loud or mousie-quiet cue cards as you sing:

Dino-loud song (sing loudly)

'Stamp, stamp, stamp your feet, stamp them on the floor.
Stamp them very noisily, like a dinosaur!'

Mousie-quiet song (sing quietly)

'Tip toe, tip toe, tip toe round the house.
Tip toe very quietly, walking like a mouse.'

Equipment

- Dino-loud and Mousie-quiet cue cards (Illustration 5)

Ground rules

- Everyone has to look at the adult holding the cue cards.

Inside information

- Demonstrate how a dinosaur stamps and a mouse tiptoes before the song starts.

Differentiation

Easier

- All the children stand still in a circle and stamp and tiptoe on the spot.

Harder

- The children can move around the room.

- Vary the order of the verses so the children need to watch the cue cards to see how to move.

Staying quiet

Game 6

Loud and quiet musical instruments

How to play

First show the children the loud (dinosaur) and quiet (mouse) cue cards and explain that the music man is going to tell them how to play their instrument. He might say play it loudly or quietly (demonstrate how this sounds with the drum). Then, choose a child to hold the drum and sing the song. Show the matching symbol as you say loudly or quietly.

'I am the music man – I come from down your way and I can play. What can you play? I play the BIG DRUM! Play it, play it LOUDLY (or QUIETLY) LOUDLY LOUDLY, play it, play it LOUDLY, play it LOUDLY!'

The drum is then passed on to the next child and the song is sung again.

Equipment

- Dino-loud and Mousie-quiet cue cards (Illustration 5)
- Drum or another musical instrument

Ground rules

- Everyone has to sit still until the music man tells them how to play.
- Everyone has to watch the adult with the loudly/quietly cue cards.

Inside information

- Hiding the cue cards behind your back until you sing (and show) the 'loudly' or 'quietly' card, helps to keep children focussed.

Differentiation

Easier

- Only one child is chosen to play each time.

Harder

- All children have an instrument.
- Use other instruments such as shakers or bells which are more challenging to play loudly/quietly.

Staying quiet

Game 7

Money Monster

How to play

The children sit in a circle. An adult sits on a chair in the middle of the circle and wears a blindfold. Put an open box or bowl behind the adult. Explain that the children have got to put their money in the Money Monster's box without waking them up. Point to one child at a time and give them a coin. They have to creep up and put it in the box as quietly as they can. If the Money Monster hears a noise, they can point to where the noise is coming from and if they point in the right place, the turn is finished and someone else can have a go.

Equipment

- Blindfold
- Box or bowl
- Coins (real or play money)

Ground rules

- Everyone has to stay quiet.
- Only children doing their best listening will get chosen to have a turn.

Inside information

- Do not hand out all of the coins at the start of the game. Only give children their coin when they have been chosen to have a turn.

Differentiation

Easier

- Put a cushion behind the Money Monster instead of a box as this makes it easier to be quiet.
- Use plastic or wooden coins.

Harder

- Put a piggy bank behind the monster.
- Use real coins.

Staying quiet

Game 8

Countdown

How to play

Show the children the two rockets and explain that we are going to count down to fly them into space, but the quiet rocket needs us to count down quietly (demonstrate this) and the loud rocket needs us to count down loudly (demonstrate this). A child is then chosen to hold a loud/quiet rocket and is told to fly it to either the moon, the star or the space station (different areas of the room). The group counts down together: 'five … four … three … two … one … blast off!'. The child then flies the rocket to the appropriate place.

Equipment

- Dino-loud and Mousie-quiet's rockets (Illustration 6)

Ground rules

- Everyone has to countdown together.

- The child has to hold the rocket still while everyone counts down.

Inside information

- Using your fingers to show the numbers as you say them will help children join in with your counting.

- This is a useful game for children to learn what loud and quiet talking sounds like, which will help them modify their own volume when talking.

Differentiation

Easier

- The rockets are put in front of the child, so they don't have to hold them during the countdown.

- Only having one destination for the rocket will reduce the language load.

Harder

- The group has to countdown from ten.

Staying quiet

Game 9

Don't wake the giant!

How to play

Make a circle of chairs. Put a large mat in the middle of the circle. Get the children to sit on the mat. An adult sits on a chair with their back to the mat and wears a blindfold. Explain to the children that they have to get back to their own chair as quietly as they can without waking the giant. A second adult touches each child on the head as a cue to let them know it is their turn to get back to their chair. If the giant hears a child moving, he can turn around and point and the turn is finished. See how many children can sit back on their chair before the giant hears and wakes up.

Equipment

- A large mat
- Blindfold

Ground rules

- Everyone has to be really quiet.
- Only one child can move at a time.
- All children must go back to their own chair.

Inside information

- This is a useful game for teaching children that they can move around the room quietly.
- You must enforce the rule that children go back to their own chair, as this will prevent arguments about who sits where.
- You can build motivation by playing a number of times and trying to beat the previous score.

Differentiation

Easier

- Move the giant's chair further away from the mat.
- Only have a small group of children starting on the mat.

Harder

- Two children move at a time.

Staying quiet

Game 10

Silent circle

How to play

The children all sit in a circle. Explain that this is a game to help the children to change places without talking. You will need photographs of all children in the group. Explain that you are going to give someone a photograph of another child. They will need to walk around the circle until they find the child, show him or her the photo and then change places with them. The next child then collects a photo and repeats until the whole group has changed places.

Equipment

- Photographs of the children in the group

Ground rules

- The adult chooses which photograph to give.

- Children can only move when they have a photograph.

- Everyone must stay quiet.

- The child must *show* the photograph without talking.

Inside information

- This is a useful game for children to learn to negotiate with each other without needing an adult to mediate.

- Make sure all children can recognise who is in the photographs.

Differentiation
Easier

- The adult gives the photograph out and then stands behind the target child.

Harder

- Have the chairs facing outwards so it is harder to scan the group.

7
Games: Sitting still

Sitting still

Game 1

Hopping frogs

How to play
Put three carpet squares or mats in the centre of the room. Choose three children to be the 'frogs' and jump around as the music plays. When the music stops the children must go and stand on a mat until the music starts again.

Equipment
- Carpet squares or mats
- Music

Ground rules
- Everyone has to stay still on their mat until the music starts again

Inside information
- This is a really good game to teach young children to manage their impulsive behaviour and wait for an adult cue. It is a good starting point for children who can't stay sitting in a group because it starts by requiring them to wait for just a second or two and builds on this.
- It helps to focus the children if the adult counts out loud using their fingers before turning the music back on, e.g. 'ready? One…two…three…four… off we go again.'
- Don't start counting straightaway. Take a moment to make sure the children are all on their mats.
- Always start with a very short wait and work on increasing the length of time they can stay still. Being able to count up to approximately 15 is a good result.
- If the adult is familiar with a signing system, then using the sign and saying 'wait' helps to focus the child.
- This game is about children learning to stay in one place and follow an adult cue. Therefore, fidgeting is allowed but children MUST stay on their mat.

Differentiation
Easier
- Children sit rather than stand on their mat.
- Make the intervals between the music shorter.

Harder
- Increase the intervals between the music so that children have to sit still for longer.

Sitting still

Game 2

'Dingle Dangle Scarecrow' song

How to play

Get the children to lie on the floor and try to be very still. Then the adult sings the 'Dingle Dangle Scarecrow' song. The lyrics for this can be found online using a search engine. Start singing the song and pause at the point just before the scarecrow jumps up. Count slowly to three, then the children can jump up and do the actions to the rest of the song.

Equipment

- None

Ground rules

- Everyone has to keep still until the adult finishes counting.

- Everyone has to stay quiet until the adult finishes counting.

Inside information

- This is a useful game to help younger children manage their impulsivity and follow an adult's lead.

- You can play the same game with other songs such as 'Sleeping Bunnies'.

- If you are going to count for longer then tell the children that you are going to make it more difficult. This will help them rise to the challenge.

Differentiation

Easier

- An adult lies with the children and does the actions at the same time.

Harder

- See if the children can wait until the count of ten.

Sitting still

Game 3

Traffic light waiting

How to play

Put the pop-up tunnel in the centre of the room. Stand next to the tunnel entrance with the stop/go sign turned to 'stop'. A child is chosen to go through the tunnel. However, they cannot go through straightaway. They have to wait until the sign is turned to 'go'.

Equipment

- Pop up tunnel

- Stop/go sign (Illustration 4)

Ground rules

- Only children who are quiet and sitting still will get chosen to have a turn in the tunnel.

- Only one child is allowed to go through the tunnel at a time. Everyone else must stay sitting still.

Inside information

- This is a really good game to teach children to wait for a turn. It is a good starting point for children who are very active or impulsive.

- Other activities can be used instead of a tunnel, but this is particularly motivating for very active children.

- It helps to focus the child if you count out loud before turning the sign round, e.g. 'You got to three last time – how long can you wait this time? One…two…three…'.

- Always start with a very short wait and work upwards, however easy it seems. This ensures the children experience success. For some impulsive children, delaying what they want to do for even five seconds is a real achievement.

- If the children are familiar with a signing system, then using the sign and saying 'wait' can help them to focus.

Differentiation

Easier

- Only wait a second or two before turning the sign around.

Harder

- Increase the amount of time that the child has to wait before they get the 'go' sign.

Sitting still

Game 4

Wake up wand

How to play

Put the chairs in a circle. Explain that you are going to play a magic spell game. All the children will have to find a space on the floor inside the circle and pretend to go to sleep. They can only wake up when the magic wand touches them. When they have been woken up, they can go back to their chair.

Equipment

- Magic wand

Ground rules

- Everyone must stay quiet and keep still.

- You can only wake up when the magic wand touches you.

- When children return to their chairs, they must still keep quiet and still.

Inside information

- Make sure there is enough room so that everyone is in a space not touching each other.

- Show all the children the wand before the game starts so they know what to expect.

- 'Wake up' the most fidgety children first.

Differentiation

Easier

- Choose a toy magic wand that makes a sound so the child can hear as well as feel when they are being woken up.

Harder

- Wake the children up one at a time very slowly.

Sitting still

Game 5

Launchpad

How to play

The children stand in a circle and sing the 'Rocket' song:

'Zoom zoom zoom

We're going to the moon

Zoom zoom zoom

We'll get there very soon!'

Then the children crouch down and say …

'In five … four … three … two …one – blast off!'

As they count down, the children have to stay still and when they say 'blast off!' they can jump up in the air.

Equipment

- None

Ground rules

- Children must not move until they hear 'blast off!'.

Inside information

- This is a useful game for impulsive children as it teaches them to wait for an adult cue before moving.

- It helps to focus the children if the adult counts out loud using their fingers.

Differentiation

Easier

- Count quickly.

Harder

- Count slowly.

- Count down from ten.

Sitting still

Game 6

Stop/go driving

How to play

All the children have a plate on the floor in front of them which is the steering wheel of their pretend car. Sing the 'driving' song and the children join and follow the actions:

'Tap your plate with your toe

hold your plate and don't let go

hold it near and hold it far

turn the key and start your car'

Then, turn the stop sign to 'go'. While the sign is on 'go' the children can drive around the room. When the adult turns the sign to 'stop', they must stop moving and stand still. The adult counts to five and then turns the sign to 'go' again and the children continue driving.

Equipment

- Paper or plastic plates
- Stop/go sign (Illustration 4)

Ground rules

- You can only move when the sign is turned to 'go'.

Inside information

- This is a useful game to teach children to manage their impulsive behaviour and wait for an adult cue.
- This game also helps children to follow instructions which are given to the whole group.

Differentiation

Easier

- Reduce the number of children 'driving' at any one time. The other children sit and wait for their turn.
- Only turn the sign to 'stop' for a second or two.

Harder

- Count up to ten before turning the sign to go again.

Sitting still

Game 7

Listen to what the sergeant says

How to play

The children walk round in a circle, following an adult and say the rhyme:

'March to the beat. March with your feet. Listen to what the sergeant says…'

When the rhyme finishes the children keep marching on the spot and listening for the adult to say one of the following commands:

'The sergeant says STOP'. (The children stop marching.)

'The sergeant says TURN AROUND.' (The children turn to face the opposite direction.)

'The sergeant says GO.' (The children start marching forwards again.)

Give two or three commands in a random order. Once the children are marching forwards again, repeat the rhyme.

Equipment

- None

Ground rules

- All children must face the same way and follow the adult.

Inside information

- Demonstrate all of the commands first, especially 'turn around'.

Differentiation
Easier

- Only do stop and go commands.

Harder

- Add ways to do the commands such as march loudly/quietly or march quickly/slowly.

Sitting still

Game 8

Animal run-around

How to play

The children sit in a circle and everyone has one of the animal cue cards to hold; there are six different animals to choose from. The adult calls the name of an animal and all the children with that cue card have to get up and walk around the outside of the circle. The adult pauses and then calls out a different animal name. The children with the next animal then have to get up and walk around while the first children sit in their places. Continue until all the animals have had a turn.

Equipment

- Animal cue cards (Illustration 7)

Ground rules

- Only children whose animal is called can get up and move around. Everyone else must sit still.

- Children must walk around the circle, not run.

Inside information

- Acknowledge that it is tricky to sit still holding a cue card. Choose a child to demonstrate how to hold the cue card and sit still.

- This is a useful game to teach children to:

  ✓ Wait for their turn.

  ✓ Follow an adult-led activity.

  ✓ Sit still while others are moving around the room.

  ✓ Think for themselves instead of copying.

Differentiation

Easier

- Adult says 'stop' and then says the new animal.

- Only have three different animals.

Harder

- Increase the number of different animals so the children have to wait longer for a turn.

Sitting still

Game 9

Distraction bubbles

How to play

This is a game to help children practise sitting still even when someone next to them is being distracting. Explain that you are going to practise sitting still, but it is going to be tricky. When the children are sitting on their mats, you are going to do something which makes it much harder for them to keep sitting still, e.g. 'I'm going to blow bubbles and they might land on your hair … they might land on your nose … they might land right next to you, but you CAN'T pop them, and you CAN'T move. You've just got to do your best sitting'. Then choose three or four children to walk around the mats and watch the 'go' sign. When the adults turns the sign to 'stop', they must sit on their mats and keep still. The adult starts the timer and blows bubbles. As soon as someone moves the timer stops. Another group of children is then chosen to see if they can beat that time.

Equipment

- Mats

- Stop/go sign (Illustration 4)

- Timer

- Bubbles

Ground rules

- The children who are watching must sit still and stay quiet. They cannot pop the bubbles.

- The grown-ups decide if someone has moved.

Inside information

- Start by saying that, 'Sometimes when children are trying to sit really well, someone next to them is a bit silly and talks to them or messes with their hair or clothes. Does that ever happen to you?' Explain that this game is to help them practise doing good sitting even when someone next to them is making it tricky.

- Make the link for the children, e.g. 'I can't believe that you sat still for a whole minute even though I was blowing bubbles on you! Now I know that you can do really good sitting on the carpet even if the other children are making it hard.'.

- This game is a really effective way to teach the concept of ignoring other children's inappropriate behaviour. Praise children in the general group if you see them trying to ignore a child who is attempting to distract them. This is a really powerful way of managing this behaviour.

Differentiation

Harder

- Use other distractions, e.g. tickling children with feather dusters. Remember to be explicit that you are trying to distract them.

Sitting still

Game 10

Statue tunnel

How to play

The children stand in a line with their legs wide apart to make a tunnel. The first child is given a ball. They must turn around and try to roll the ball through the statue tunnel. The other children must stay still to let the ball pass through. The child at the end of the tunnel then collects the ball and comes to the front. Repeat until everyone has had a turn.

Equipment

- Soft ball

Ground rules

- The adult chooses who goes first.

- Children have to stand still even if the ball touches them.

- Only the child at the end of the line can collect the ball.

Inside information

- Demonstrate how to roll the ball first.

- Make sure children know who is first and last in the line.

- This is a game for smaller groups of children. If you are working with a whole class then choose teams of six children and see which group completes the activity fastest.

Differentiation

Easier

- Choose a small tennis ball.

- Only four to six children make the statue tunnel.

Harder

- Time them and try to beat their previous score.

8

Games: Listening to all of the words

Listening to all of the words

Game 1

Matching instruments

How to play

Put one set of instruments in front of the child. The other set should be kept in the bag. You play one of the instruments from within the bag and the child has to select and play the one that matches. Then, take the instrument out of the bag to show the child that they are the same.

Equipment

- Two matching sets of three or four instruments
- A bag or other barrier

Ground rules

- You must listen to the sound before you touch the instruments.

Inside information

- If a child finds it really difficult to match the instruments using sound alone, start by taking the instrument out of the bag before playing it so that it becomes a visual matching activity. Draw the child's attention to the sound and, when the child is confident at this, try again with just the sound.

- The children will want to play the instruments and it is probably wise to let them get this out of their system first! With a small group, pass each instrument around so each child can play it once before the activity. With a large group, let the child have a quick chance to play all the instruments before their turn.

Differentiation

Easier

- Just have a choice of two instruments.

Harder:

- Increase the numbers of instruments the child has to choose from.

- Use similar sounding instruments.

- Play a sequence of two or more instruments. The child then has to select the right instruments AND put them in the right order. (TIP: This is also a really good early literacy activity because it teaches children to remember and reassemble a sequence of sounds.)

Listening to all of the words

Game 2

Actions to sounds

How to play

Show children two different musical instruments. Tell them that every time they hear instrument one (e.g. bells) they have to walk around the circle and every time they hear instrument two (e.g. drum) they have to jump. Then play each instrument for varying lengths of time, swapping between them. The children have to change actions when the sound changes.

Equipment

- Musical instruments

Ground rules

- Everyone has to stay quiet.

Inside information

- Practise the two actions first.

- Make sure you choose musical instruments which sound very different.

Differentiation

Easier

- Choose two children to do the game first. The other children stay sitting down and wait for their turn.

Harder

- Swap between instruments more frequently.

- Introduce a third instrument and action, e.g. they have to clap when they hear the shaker.

Listening to all of the words

Game 3

Listening for 'go'

How to play

You will need a marble run or similar activity. The activity needs to be very motivating for the children. A child is chosen to have a turn and is given the marble but cannot put it down the marble run until you say 'go'.

Equipment

- A marble run or equivalent

Ground rules

- Only children who are sitting still and not shouting out will get chosen to have a turn with the marble run.

- You MUST wait to hear 'go' before you put the marble down the run.

Inside information

- As well as being a good listening game, this is a good activity to teach children to wait for an adult signal. It is a good starting point for managing the behaviour of children who are very active or impulsive.

- It may help to focus the child if you count out loud before saying 'go', e.g. 'You got to five last time – how long can you wait this time? One … two … three …'.

- Always start with a very short wait and work upwards, however easy it seems, to ensure the children experience success.

- If you are familiar with a signing system, then using the sign and saying 'wait' can help to focus the child.

Differentiation

Easier

- Only wait a second or two before saying 'go'.

- Say 'ready … steady … GO!' to keep the child focussed.

- Use the stop/go sign to help focus the children.

Harder

- Increase the amount of time that the child has to wait before you say 'go'.

- Whisper 'go' but warn the child that you are going to make it harder and they will have to listen very carefully.

Listening to all of the words

Game 4

Changing places

How to play

The children sit in a circle. Explain that you are going to say the names of two children. Those children must stand up and change places. Remind the children that you might say their name more than once so that even if they have had a turn they need to keep listening.

Equipment

- None

Ground rules

- You can only move when your name is called.

- You must stay quiet while you are moving so that other children can listen for their names.

Inside information

- If children are reluctant to move, they may need an adult to help them change places.

Differentiation

Easier

- Look at the child as you say their name.

Harder

- Say the names of some children several times in quick succession to help them learn to keep listening even when they have had a turn.

- Introduce a new rule where you occasionally say the name of the group or class and everyone has to change places.

Listening to all of the words

Game 5

Old Macdonald's farm

How to play

Put a set of the animal cue cards up on different walls in the room. The children stand in a group in the middle of the circle and sing 'Old Macdonald had a farm':

'Old Macdonald had a farm, e-i-e-i-o

And on that farm he had a …'

Pause for a few seconds and then say the name of an animal. The children have to run to stand by that picture. When they are all standing in the right place, sing the rest of that verse.

'With moo moo here, and a moo moo there. Here a moo. There a moo. Everywhere a moo moo. Old Macdonald had a farm, e i e i o'.

Then the children return to the middle of the room and the song starts again.

Equipment

- A set of animal cue cards (Illustration 7)

Ground rules

- Everyone has to come to the middle of the room to sing the first part of the song.

Inside information

- Make sure the children can recognise the animals in the pictures.

Differentiation

Easier

- Only choose three different animals.
- Start by showing the cue card while you say the animal name.

Harder

- Do the animal noise instead of the name, e.g. 'an animal that says moo'.

Listening to all of the words

Game 6

Farmyard swap

How to play

The children sit in a circle. The adult shows the children each of the animal cue cards, says the name and talks about what noise it makes. Each child is then given a cue card to hold. The adult makes an animal noise, e.g. 'woof' or 'moo', and all the children holding the corresponding cue card have to stand up and swap places. Remind the children that you might make their noise more than once so that even if they have had a turn they need to keep listening.

Equipment

- Animal cue cards (Illustration 7)

Ground rules

- You can only move when you hear your animal noise.

- You must stay quiet while you are moving so that other children can listen for their sound.

Inside information

- If children are reluctant to move, they may need an adult to help them change places.

- If you are doing this with a small group of children, you will need an empty chair in the circle, so the children have a space to move to.

- This is a great game to reinforce other topic vocabulary too. Use the same rules but choose cue cards of words relevant to the group's topic, e.g. for minibeasts use pictures of a butterfly, a spider, a caterpillar, a ladybird, a worm and a grasshopper.

Differentiation

Easier

- Use the animal name instead of the animal sound.

Harder

- Make two animal noises and both sets of children have to change places.

- Introduce a rule where you sometimes say 'farmyard' and all the children have to change places.

Listening to all of the words

Game 7

Who is hungry?

How to play

The children sit in a circle. Show the cue cards of the cat, dog, duck and cow (see Illustration 7), model the noise each makes and put them in the middle of the circle. Then explain that all the animals are hungry and the children need to help them find their food. Show each food card to demonstrate the dog wants a bone, the cat wants a fish, the duck wants some bread, and the cow wants some grass. Put the food cards in the middle of the circle. Then sing the 'Who is hungry?' song while the children pass the plate around the circle and join in with the words.

'The animals are hungry,

the animals are hungry,

the animals are hungry,

who will have some food?'

When the song finishes, the child holding the plate has to listen while you make one of the animal noises. The child then has to find the food that the animal will like, put it on the plate and give it to the animal. The group then sings the song again until each animal has got their food.

Equipment

- Animal cue cards (Illustration 7)
- Animal food cue cards (Illustration 8)
- Plate

Ground rules

- Everyone must pass the plate until the song finishes.
- Only the child holding the plate can feed the animals.

Inside information

- Appropriate soft animal toys can be used instead of cue cards.
- An adult might need to help children pass the plate on.

Differentiation
Easier

- Say the animal name instead of making the noise when the song finishes.
- Only have a choice of two animals.

Listening to all of the words

Game 8

Feeding time at the farm

How to play

Put the animal cue cards out in front of the children. Explain the animals are hungry and the children need to feed them but they will have to listen very carefully to all of the words so they know what to do. Then choose one child to have the first turn. Ask them to give some food to an animal, e.g. 'Give the <u>grass</u> to the <u>cow</u>'; 'give the <u>bone</u> to the <u>dog</u>'. Continue until everyone has had a turn.

Equipment

- Animal cue cards (Illustration 7)

- Animal food cue cards (Illustration 8)

Ground rules

- Children need to listen to ALL the words first and then feed the animals.

Inside information

- This is a useful activity for children who only listen to the first part of an instruction because they have to listen to all of the words to get it right.

- Make sure you do not give children any extra clues, e.g. giving the instruction in two steps.

Differentiation

Easier

- Use toy animals and play food instead of pictures.

- Make the food choices predictable.

- Use gestures to support your language.

Harder

- Make unpredictable or silly food choices, e.g. 'give the bone to the duck'.

Listening to all of the words

Game 9

Sorting the washing

How to play

Tie up a washing line between two chairs. Place a basket and a pile of clothes next to the line. Explain to the children that they are going to sort the washing out and they will need to listen to ALL the words so they know what to do. Then ask the children to get a particular item of clothing and either put it in the basket or on the washing line, e.g. 'put the <u>sock</u> on the <u>line</u>' or 'put the <u>hat</u> in the <u>basket</u>'. Repeat until all the children have had a turn.

Equipment

- Washing line and pegs
- Washing basket
- Assorted doll or baby clothes

Ground rules

- Children need to listen to ALL the words first and then sort the washing.

Inside information

- Let all the children practise with the pegs the first time you play this game.
- This is a useful activity for children who only listen to the first part of an instruction because they have to listen to all of the words to get it right.
- Make sure you do not give children any extra clues, e.g. giving the instruction in two steps.

Differentiation
Easier

- Only put two items of clothing out at a time.

Harder

- Have different sized items of clothing and introduce big and little, e.g. 'put the <u>big jumper</u> in the <u>basket</u>'.

Listening to all of the words

Game 10

Seaside name story

How to play

Read the name story (Appendix 11) and insert the names of the children in the group. When the children hear their name, they have to stand up and sit down again. When the children hear 'everyone' then they all have to stand up and sit down.

Equipment

- A copy of the name story (Appendix 11)

Ground rules

- Everyone has to stay quiet while they listen to the story.

- You can only stand up when you hear your name.

Inside information

- Make sure you include each child's name more than once and be explicit that they need to keep listening for their name even once they have had a turn.

- This is a useful activity for children who need individual instructions because they don't understand that 'everyone' includes them too.

- Wait for each child to sit back down before continuing with the story.

Differentiation

Easier

- Look at the child as you say their name.

Harder

- Insert more than one child's name into a space in the story.

9

Supporting parents to create a listening-friendly home

Listening skills develop from birth. Children's experiences in the early months of life can help them to develop good listening skills that will give them a secure foundation for their learning in their Early Years setting. This chapter is designed to give Early Years practitioners advice and resources that they can use to support the families they work with.

Advice for 0–12 months

This is a crucial stage for listening because it is the time when many of the foundation skills, such as eye contact and turn taking, develop. Here are our key strategies for supporting babies to develop their early listening skills. (These are summarised in Appendix 6, which has been designed to show key ages and stages linked to specific strategies to support children at each stage.)

Learning to make eye contact

Encouraging eye contact helps babies to focus on the person who is talking and shows them that faces are an interesting and rewarding place to look. It will also give them lots of extra useful information that will help them to understand what you are saying to them.

Practical advice to give to parents:

- Get down to the baby's eye level when talking to them.
- Encourage parents to look at their baby when they breast or bottle feed them.
- Avoid using screen time for babies who are under one year old, e.g. phones/tablets/TV.
- Advise parents to choose a rear-facing pushchair or buggy so the baby can focus on the parent's face.

Developing their focus and interest in voices

Babies rarely spend time in quiet environments and will often have to listen to people talking to them with many competing noises. A speaker's voices need to be 15–20 decibels louder than the background noise in order for a baby to focus on it. Reducing the background noise will help both babies and children to do this.

Practical advice to give to parents:

- Reduce background noise as much as possible, especially when talking or playing with the baby.

- Turn the television off when no-one is watching it to reduce the noise levels and limit visual distractions.
- Sing songs and nursery rhymes to the baby from birth.
- Use lots of positive facial expressions when you are talking to the baby.
- Use the baby's name from birth and include it in rhymes and songs.
- Call the baby's name and wait for them to look before speaking.

Taking turns with sounds

Learning to listen to and respond to sounds is a foundation skill that will later help children to take turns in conversation. Taking turns with sounds helps children to learn that only one person talks at a time and the other person stays quiet, so they can listen until it is their turn to talk again.

Practical advice to give to parents:

- Look at the baby when you are talking to them so they can pick up your non-verbal cues. This will help them to learn to take turns.
- Copy the sounds the baby makes to you.
- Make eye contact and give the baby time to respond in some way before you say something new.

Supporting listening in children older than 12 months

Helping young children to share attention with you

Babies and very young children tend to focus just on things that they are interested in. They can be easily distracted and move very quickly to anything new that takes their attention. Learning to share attention with another person so that they can jointly focus on a shared interest is a key step to developing early listening skills. Following the child's lead when you play with them will help them to understand that you share their enjoyment and they are then more likely to stay focussed on an activity for longer and include you in their play. Using simple language with them as you play will make sure that child hears language that is relevant to the play activity.

Key tips to following a child's lead in play

Let them choose what to play with:

- Try not to have too many choices, e.g. no more than two or three toys.
- Let the child choose the toy or activity – don't jump in and make the choice for the child.
- Let them choose how to play with the toys, even if it isn't the 'proper' way to play with them!

Watch them and see what they do:

- Watch carefully to see what the child is doing and copy their actions or sounds.
- Remember the child may not use words. They may use a look, facial expression, a sound or reach for your hand.

- Make sure you are at the same level as the child and you are facing each other.
- Move with the child as they explore the toys.

Wait for a response:

- Don't jump in and start talking too quickly – wait and listen first.
- Don't worry about silences – give the child time to respond.

Comment on what you see:

- Comment on what the child is looking at or doing using simple language and short phrases, e.g. 'cars crash!' or 'all fall down'.
- Point and gesture at the same time as saying the words.
- Slow down – don't feel you need to rush or use lots of words when you are talking to the child.
- Keeping your language simple will give the child an easier model to copy.
- Repeat words and phrases lots of times as you play. Children need to listen to words many times to help them understand and then use the words.

Play example for sharing attention and following a child's lead

---

Bubbles

Playing with bubbles with the child can help them to learn to make eye contact and take turns as well as encouraging them to communicate with you to keep the game going for longer.

- Get down to the child's level so they can see your face easily.
- Hold the bubbles near your face.
- Call the child's name to gain their attention.
- Say 'look, bubbles!' and blow some bubbles in to the air between you.
- As they reach for the bubbles say 'pop!' as they catch them.
- Say and gesture 'all gone!' when all the bubbles have disappeared.
- Wait until the child indicates that they would like some more bubbles. They might do this by looking at you, reaching for the bubbles, pointing or making a noise.
- Say 'more' or 'more bubbles' as you blow again.

You can find advice for parents on helping young children to share attention in a photocopiable handout in Appendix 7.

Managing screen time

Technology has many fantastic benefits for children. It is possible for children to learn new things from screens, but research tells us that small children learn more efficiently and meaningfully from real-life interactions with people and things. Screens can't prepare a toddler for the finely-tuned, subtle turn taking of interaction in the real world. For example, screens only give a two-dimensional experience of the world; they do not always expect you to respond and they do not vary their response if you don't listen to them!

Here are our top tips for practitioners to share with parents and carers of toddlers to help them get the technology balance right so that they give children the best opportunities of learning to listen and to interact:

- **Manage screen time.** Treat technology as you would any other environment a child spends time in and make sure you put limits on it. Adults need to be the ones who are in charge of screen time. Make sure that you consider all the screens a child experiences – television tablets, smart phones all count towards the total!

- **Join in!** You being part of their learning will help them to learn much more effectively. Watch a programme with them and talk about what you have seen. Look for interactive games that you can play on the tablet together – it will really help them to get the most out of the screen time.

- **Be aware of background noise.** In order to develop both their listening and their speaking skills, children need to hear adults talking against a background of silence at least some of the time. Noise from the television, radio or electronic games can really get in the way. If you are not watching it or listening to it then turning it off will help make it a better environment for listening.

- **No-screen bedrooms.** Research tells us that as little as two hours of screen time a day can increase the risk of sleep difficulties in children. Tired children find it hard to listen and learn. You can help by making bedrooms a no-screen zone and making the last hour before bedtime a time for listening to stories and talking rather than watching a screen.

- **Be a good model.** Show children what you want them to do. If you want them to look at you when you are talking rather than look at a screen, then it is important that you look up from your phone or laptop when they speak to you. Children learn best through imitation so make sure you are showing them the behaviour you want to see.

Advice on managing screen time for parents is available as a handout in Illustration 10.

Sharing the approach with parents

We aim for the children we work with to be good listeners in every situation. They are more likely to generalise their new skills if parents understand the importance of good listening and can encourage their children to carry out the rules at home too.

Parents may not be aware of the challenges that children face when listening as part of a group and the impact that poor listening can have on their child's learning. Appendix 7 summarises the approach for parents and gives you information that you can share about the support for listening within your Early Years setting.

Appendix 8 contains two games for each listening rule that parents can play at home to support the intervention that you are doing with children.

10
How to talk so children will listen

What adults say and how they say it can make a real difference to how well children listen. Children can stop listening for a number of reasons:

- They do not realise the adult is talking to them.
- There are too many competing distractions which stop children focussing on the speaker.
- The adult talks for too long, so children cannot remember everything that has been said.
- The children do not have time to process what has been said before the adult starts speaking again.
- The adult uses ambiguous language, which children can interpret literally.
- The adult uses words that the child does not yet understand.
- The adult uses a 'trigger phrase', e.g. 'it's nearly snack time so wash your hands', which impulsive children respond to immediately and do not listen to the rest of the instruction.

Here are 10 ways to talk so that children will listen:

1. **Call their name and wait for them to look towards you.**
   Young children have single-channelled attention. So, if they are not looking at you then they are probably not listening. Calling their name and waiting for them to turn towards you helps them to be ready to focus on your words when you start speaking.

2. **Get down to their level.**
   Getting down so that you face the child at the same level as them will help them to focus on you and screen out other people and activity in the room.

3. **Reduce background noise before you speak.**
   Children find it far harder to screen out background noise than adults do. Reducing the noise before you speak will help them to focus on your words. Try clapping a rhythm, modelling actions to copy or using a sound cue such as a rainmaker toy or a tambourine so that the children learn the signal that you need them to be quiet so that you can talk. This reinforces the expectation that children are quiet when adults are talking and also helps children to recognise that stopping and being quiet helps them to listen.

4. **Reduce the load.**
   Using instructions that are short and easy to understand will make it easier for children to listen. Compare: 'In a couple of minutes, we will have to tidy up and have our snack so before we go to the toilet, I want all the toys back in the boxes' with: 'Tidy up time.'

5. Tell, don't ask.

Children can often misinterpret instructions that are phrased as a question or a choice that they can say no to. If you are giving a child an instruction, then make sure you are not giving them a choice. For example:

Instead of:	Try:
'Would you like to come inside now?'	'Time to come inside.'
'Shall we give someone else a turn on the bike now?'	'Harry's turn on the bike now.'
'Can you come and do your painting with me?'	'Painting now.'

6. Keep it concrete.

Figures of speech, e.g. 'you're on fire today' or 'Mummy's running a bit late', can make it hard for children to listen and understand what you mean.

7. Use pauses.

Many young children can only process one piece of information at a time. If an adult starts talking again too soon, they will struggle to keep listening. Using pauses before giving a new instruction allows children time to process one thing that you have said before they need to listen to the next.

8. Avoid before and after.

'Before' and 'after' change the order of an instruction without changing the order of the words, e.g. 'Before we go outside we need to put our coats on'. As adults we understand that the word 'before' means that the child needs to put their coat on first and *then* go outside. However, a child who does not understand 'before' will just follow the sentence order and go outside first. This makes 'before' and 'after' very challenging concepts to understand and typically-developing children do not acquire these concepts until about six years of age. Using 'first' and 'next' with pauses will help children to listen to and carry out two-part instructions successfully:

Instead of:	Try:
'Before we sit on the carpet put your models on the shelf.'	'First, models on shelf. Next, carpet.'
'We can go outside after you have finished your picture.'	'First, picture. Next, outside.'

9. Watch out for trigger phrases.

Trigger phrases contain exciting information which stop children listening to anything else you say. Examples of trigger phrases are:

> 'Line up at the door.'
> 'It's nearly playtime.'
> 'It's snowing.'

The rule about managing trigger phrases is to only say them when there is nothing else left to be said. If you join them to another instruction, it is highly likely that many impulsive children will only respond to the trigger phrase and you will then need to refocus them and repeat your instruction.

10. Help children to understand that 'everyone' includes them.

Some children in Early Years settings do not respond to instructions which are given to the whole group. This is because they have not yet learnt that they are part of 'everyone' and that instructions which are given to all children apply to them too. For these children, it can be helpful to name them explicitly in whole group instructions, e.g. 'Everyone, and Matthew, come and sit on the carpet'. Linking their name with the word 'everyone' will help them to learn this concept.

11

Helping children to listen in every context

Teaching children a new skill in a structured activity is the easy part, but getting them to use that skill in real life situations can be more of a challenge. Listening is no different. Showing good listening skills in a small group is no use at all if all the new skills disappear as soon as they are back in their usual learning environment. However, there are strategies you can use both within the group and in everyday teaching which will help children to generalise their new listening skills.

Strategies to use in your listening group

- **Be explicit about the target behaviour needed to get a turn.**

   At the beginning of each game, be clear about what the children need to do in order to get a turn. Be consistent in expecting this behaviour, e.g. 'I can choose you Liam because you are looking at me now'. You can use this principle both in the group and in other turn taking activities throughout the day.

- **Be explicit about why children are not getting chosen for a turn.**

   Children will generally want to have a turn in the game but may not yet have the insight to understand how to modify their behaviour to get chosen. You can help them by giving them explicit feedback and a realistic target to aim for, e.g. 'Max, I'd love to choose you for this game, but can I choose you if you are talking to Pari?' This lets them know that you want to choose them and helps them make the link between the behaviour and getting chosen. Then, give them an attainable target behaviour, e.g. 'I'm going to be watching you and when you are quiet I might be able to give you a turn'. Then, choose them as soon as they show the behaviour you have asked for and make the link again by saying 'I can choose you now! Why can I choose you?'

- **Be unpredictable when choosing who has a turn.**

   If everyone gets a turn in a predictable order, regardless of how they are behaving, children soon learn that they will eventually get a turn and therefore there is less incentive to show the target behaviour you are looking for. If groups are run in this way, then children also switch off once they have had a turn as they know that they will not get chosen again. Make sure that children know you will choose children who are showing you good listening and that even if they have had a turn already, if they keep listening they could get chosen again. This may mean that at the end of the group, some children will have had more turns than others, but all of the children will have been more motivated to keep listening.

- **Make links to other situations.**

   There is something very powerful in the children knowing that the adult has seen them doing good listening and will be expecting to see it again in other situations. You can exploit this by taking a few moments at the end of the group to tell them what you have seen them do really well and help them think of other times that it would be good to show that listening behaviour, e.g. 'Luka, you did a fantastic job of sitting still then! I'm going to watch to see if you can do that brilliant sitting at story time.'.

Strategies to use throughout the day

Using photographs

Using photographs in class helps to make the rules more meaningful to children and reminds them of what they are able to do. Seeing a photograph of themselves showing a good listening rule can support them to understand what they need to do in a new situation. Here are some creative ways to use photographs with the children you work with:

Photographs to illustrate the rules

Take photographs of the children carrying out each of the four rules and display these alongside the listening cue cards. It is very important to take photographs of good listening in more than one context, e.g. sitting still on the carpet, sitting still in a focussed activity, as this helps children to generalise the skills that they have learnt and recognise that good listening is important in all situations. Choose children who find a rule particularly challenging to be the person to demonstrate that rule in the photograph. This is a really positive way of helping those children to understand the target behaviour you are looking for and will also build their self-esteem, e.g. 'Don't forget, Kieron, your photo is here to show everyone how to sit on the carpet. Can you keep showing everyone?'

Photographs for individual children

Photographs can also help individual children who find listening a challenge. A template for a listening fan can be found in Illustration 11. Illustrate this fan with photos of the child carrying out each rule. The adult can then show a photograph to remind the child of the target behaviour at the beginning of any activity. They can also use the fan to silently refocus a child on to the task. This is much less disruptive than having to talk to them to refocus their attention while another adult is leading the activity. The fan can also be used by other adults in different environments and at home to help children generalise their good listening. It is important to remember that the fan is a resource for adults to use rather than being given to the child who would be distracted by holding it.

Photographs when children are sitting together

Sitting on the floor in a group can be challenging – children can be easily distracted and can distract other children. Organising who sits together and where children can sit is time consuming. A helpful way to reduce the need for negotiation and to improve children's listening in these situations is to assemble the group so that every child has a space, the right children are sitting together, and everyone is looking at the adult leading the group. Then take a photograph which will become your 'carpet time map'. You can either display it next to the seating area or use it as a screensaver if you have an interactive whiteboard. This then becomes the 'rule' for where children sit every day. This reduces the need for discussion and also helps to generalise their good listening when other adults lead the activities.

Reducing noise levels

Background noise can have a significant impact on any child's ability to listen in Early Years settings. In order for children to be able to screen out background noise effectively, adults need to be speaking at a level 15–20 decibels above the background noise. Typical Early Years settings are busy and noisy places. If adults try to give instructions while competing with those noise levels, then children will be unlikely to focus on what they are saying. It is good practice to use a non-verbal method of establishing quiet such as clapping a rhythm that children can copy or using a sound maker, e.g. bells. This also helps children that need to learn to stop what they are doing in order to listen to what the adult is saying. It is also helpful in other contexts to be explicit that you are waiting for children to be quiet before you can speak, e.g. 'I want to tell you what we are going to do next, but I can't because some people are still talking so I am going to wait until everyone's quiet'.

Think about seating

Children in Early Years are most often expected to listen when they are sitting on the floor. This is very challenging for many children for the following reasons:

- Sitting on the floor without any back support requires a high level of core stability that some children have not yet developed. This means they are either having to work hard at sitting upright, leaving less capacity to listen to you, or they lean on another child or roll and lie on the floor.
- Many young children find it hard to organise themselves in relation to other people and objects. This means they can invade the personal space of other children by sitting too close to them which distracts both themselves and the other child.
- Sitting on the carpet can increase the distractions around them, e.g. texture of carpet, their own and other children's shoes and clothes and toys and equipment within reach of the carpet area.

What can you do to help?

- Reduce the time that children are expected to sit and listen.
- Make sure that the children who find listening the biggest challenge are sitting at the front of the group, closest to the adult.
- Give all children a designated space to sit on. This helps children to organise their personal space more effectively. This can be using carpet squares or by using the 'carpet time map' idea.
- Timetable carpet time activities for the period after children have been engaging in physically active play, preferably outside.
- Consider using chairs during adult-led activities for children who find sitting still a real challenge as this will both support core stability and organise their personal space.

Managing distractions

Early Years settings are designed to give children lots of choice and exciting opportunities for play. However, some young children are distracted very easily by all the competing demands on their attention and find it hard to sustain their focus on a particular activity for any length of time. Other children can become overwhelmed by the options open to them and find it difficult to choose an activity independently.

What can you do to help?

- Reduce the choice when appropriate. Put away toys that are not part of the activity. Do not let children see new or exciting activities until it is time to do them.

- Using photographs of children to 'check in' and 'check out' of activities can help them to stay focussed for longer and support children who would otherwise flit between activities.

- At the beginning of adult-directed activities, be explicit about the possible distractions and set the children a challenge by telling them what behaviour you will be expecting from them, e.g. 'Kaylee will be choosing some children to go and work with her. Can you still keep looking at me even when Kaylee is calling someone out?'

- A choice board (Appendix 9) using photographs of the activities available can support anxious children to make a choice and keep them focussed when carrying out their chosen activities. An adult can use this resource to show a child the available activities and they can then choose a photograph of the first thing they will do. With young children, support them to choose just one activity. With Reception-age children, use Appendix 10 so they can make a choice of 'this activity first, then this'.

Consider children's attention levels

Most young children have single-channelled attention. This means that they need to look at the speaker in order to listen to them. By the time children start school, they may have started to develop dual-channelled attention which means they can listen to an adult and carry out an activity at the same time. However, for most children this will still be an inconsistent skill. They will find it much easier to listen if they are looking at the speaker.

What can you do to help?

- When you are playing with children, try to follow their lead. Watch what they are looking at and are interested in and comment on what they can see and what they are doing. They will be much more able to listen to language that matches what they see and do. Copying their actions as you play together will help them to sustain their focus for longer.

- When you need children to listen, calling their name and waiting for them to look at you will help them to transfer their attention to you and focus on that they are saying.

- When it is really import that a child listens to you, you may need to make sure they are not holding anything or engaged in an activity which will distract them.

12
What's the evidence?

Why do so many children find it so hard to listen?

As already discussed, learning to listen and focus on another person successfully requires children to use several different skills. Similarly, it is not likely that one factor alone is the reason why so many children find listening a challenge. The decline in children's ability to listen is likely to be the result of a complex interaction of cultural changes. Factors which might be relevant are:

- **The amount of time children spend facing a screen.**
  The rise in availability of screen-based entertainment has coincided with increasing numbers of children who have not yet developed the listening skills they need when starting school. Every hour children spend facing a screen is an hour less for them to spend in interaction with another person. Robust listening skills can only develop if children have many opportunities to practise using them in real life situations. A report from Ofcom (2017) indicated that pre-school children were spending more than four hours a day engaged in screen-based activities and that 58% of three-to-four-year-olds owned their own tablet.

- **Changes in the way children play and learn to interact.**
  The rise in screen-based entertainment has been mirrored by a decline in more traditional play activities. Children playing together are now likely to watch a screen or play a computer game rather than to engage in imaginative play, which requires them interact, negotiate with and listen to another person.

- **Background noise levels when babies and children are learning to talk.**
  Typical early life experiences of many young children include very high levels of background noise. This can be from television, radio, electronic devices used by other members of the family or noise from busy childcare settings. All children find it harder than adults to screen out background noise in order to listen. Noisy environments can make it hard for children to focus on voices. Taking part in conversations when there is a lot of background noise can also mean that children get used to speaking over other people and this can affect their ability to stay quiet and take turns in a conversation.

However, the vast majority of children do have the ability to listen when given the opportunity and experiences to help them learn these skills. Our work with children has consistently shown the impact of explicitly teaching them to listen.

Evidence of impact

When delivering intervention in school and nursery settings, we use the listening rating scale to evaluate outcomes for each group of children.

Teaching staff rate the listening of the children that they are working with before and after the intervention. (See Chapter 3 for more information on evaluating children's listening skills.) To maximise objectivity, when teaching staff re-evaluate the children's listening, they do not have access to their original ratings. The listening rating scale used by staff can be found in Appendix 1.

We use children's listening scores to classify them in the following way:

- A score of below 8 indicates a **severe listening difficulty**
- A score between 8–12 indicates **a moderate listening difficulty**
- A score between 12–16 indicates **adequate listening skills**

We have now worked with over 3300 children. Over 1000 of these have been in Early Years. The graphs below show the proportion of children in each category before and after intervention as rated by the teaching staff who work with them.

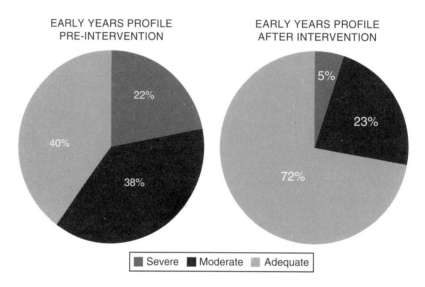

DIAGRAM 1 Evaluation of 1034 Early Years children before and after listening intervention

Measuring the impact of intervention

In order to establish that the children were making progress because of intervention rather than just exposure to the learning environment, we worked with three classes of Reception-aged children over the course of a term in 2017. All of the children's listening was rated by their teachers at the start, middle and end of the term. All of the children took part in a weekly session using the games and activities outlined in this book. One class took part in the first half term. The other two classes took part in the second half of the term. Delivering the approach at different times in the term allowed us to see whether the children made accelerated progress after intervention. The 45-minute session was delivered alongside the teacher each week for six weeks. The numbers of children rated as having adequate listening in each of the intervention cohorts is shown in Diagram 2.

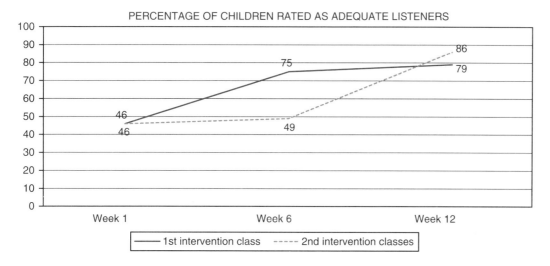

PERCENTAGE OF CHILDREN RATED AS ADEQUATE LISTENERS

DIAGRAM 2 Percentage of children rated as adequate listeners

The results showed that both cohorts of children made some progress in each six-week period, but the progress was significantly accelerated when children had participated in the intervention. The results also showed that the progress made by the first cohort that received the intervention was sustained and built upon without any further direct intervention taking place.

These results show that children can make sustained and significant progress in learning to listen with a small amount of targeted input. Once children understand what good listening means, and have explicit and consistent expectations placed on them, they are both motivated and able to change their own behaviour in order to listen effectively.

13
Case histories

When children find it hard to listen it can affect both their ability to interact with others and their ability to learn effectively. Many children do not have the early life experiences which allow them to develop robust listening skills but given the right support they can learn this skill. Our experience has taught us that with a small amount of targeted input children can learn to listen and this can have a huge impact on their ability to learn and succeed.

CASE HISTORY: OLIVER

Oliver was just four when we worked with his Reception class. He was rated by his teacher as having severe listening difficulties, scoring only four on the listening rating scale. He found it difficult to comply with any whole class activity and would either disrupt the learning of other children by repeatedly demanding the attention of the adult(s) leading the lesson, or would remove himself from the classroom. Oliver's language was significantly delayed.

At the beginning of the listening intervention, Oliver wanted to participate in games but couldn't wait for his turn. He constantly said 'me, me, me' and, when this didn't work, tried to gain our attention by tapping or tugging us. We were explicit with Oliver about the behaviour he needed to show in order to be chosen for a turn. It took two or three sessions for Oliver to develop some awareness and ability to control his own behaviour. Once he was able to sit still and stay quiet for a brief period, he could be chosen to have a turn. We were always explicit about why we could choose him, for example 'I can choose you now Oliver, because you are being quiet'.

By the end of the intervention, Oliver had developed some insight and control over his impulsive behaviour. He responded to explicit reminders about the listening rules at the beginning of a whole-class activity, and although he continued to find it difficult to listen to all of the words, his more compliant behaviour had a positive impact on the listening environment for the rest of the class.

CASE HISTORY: CHLOE

Chloe was four and had a diagnosis of global developmental delay. At the start of the intervention she presented as a very passive child. Her teacher rated her as having significant difficulties looking at the person who is talking, and listening to all of the words. However, she scored well for sitting still and staying quiet. Because Chloe's attention was single channelled, teaching her to look at the speaker was a key skill for her to learn as this helped her to recognise the focus for an activity. Looking at the adult increased her chances of listening to the instructions. Chloe became a more active participant during intervention and by the end was putting up her hand to be chosen for a turn. Her ability to look at adults and other children in the group also improved. This helped her at other times during the school day, both during adult-led activities in class, and when playing with other children.

CASE HISTORY: KAI

Kai was three when he participated in a listening group with three other children at nursery. He was learning to follow an adult's lead when working one to one but wasn't yet able to participate in group activities. This small group intervention helped him to move from only sharing attention with an adult, to being able to wait for his turn alongside other children. This is an essential skill for school where children are expected to share attention with others and comply with adult-led activities. Kai learnt the structure of each session and was helped by explicit feedback about how he needed to wait such as 'Jack's turn now, Kai next'. By the end of the intervention, Kai knew he couldn't be chosen first every time and was able to wait until two other children were chosen before he had a turn. Although this sounds like a small step, Kai was then able to generalise these skills in order to participate in other adult-led group activities at nursery and also comply with the listening rules at story time at the end of the morning.

References

Bercow, J. (2008), *Review of Services for Children and Young People (0–19) with Speech, Language and Communication Needs*. http://dera.ioe.ac.uk/8405/7/7771-dcsf-bercow_Redacted.pdf

Boyd, S. and Clarke, H. (2011), *Sentence Trouble*. The Communication Trust.

Christakis, D. A. Zimmerman, F. J. DiGiuseppe, D. L. and McCarty, C. A. (2004), 'Early television exposure and subsequent attentional problems in children'. *Journal of Paediatrics*, 113(4) 708–13.

Evans Schmidt, M. Pempek, T. A. Kirkorian, H. L. Frankenfield Lund, A. and Anderson, D. R. (2008), 'The effects of background television on the toy play behavior of very young children'. *Child Development*, July/August 2008, 79(4), p.1137–1151

Greenfield, N (2007), 'Testing 1, 2, 3. Can you hear me?'. *Times Educational Supplement Scotland* 19 October, 2007.

Harries, J. (2013), *Getting Ready for Phonics*. London: Bloomsbury, p.129.

Hastings, N. and Chantry-Wood, K. (2000), 'Spacing for learning in primary classrooms: Bridging the gaps'. Paper presented at the British Educational Research Association Conference.

Hollich, G. Newman, R. S. Jusczyk, P. W. (2005), 'Infants' Use of Synchronized Visual Information to Separate Streams of Speech'. *Child Development* Volume 76, Issue 3, Pages 598–613

ICAN (2006), The Cost to the Nation of Children's Poor Communication. *ICAN Talk series* – issue 2. www.ican.org.uk

Kirkorian, H. L. Pempek, T. A. Murphy, L. A. Evans Schmidt, M. and Anderson, D. R. (2009), 'The impact of background television on parent-child interaction'. *Child Development*, Sep/Oct 2009, 80(5), p.1350–9

Maxwell, L. E. and Evans, G. W. (2004), 'Impact of classroom noise on reading'. Paper presented at 147th Acoustical Society of America meeting.

Murkoff, H. Eisenberg, A. Hathaway, S. (2004), *What to Expect in the First Year* (2nd edition). Great Britain: Simon and Schuster UK Ltd

Ofcom. (2017), 'Children and Parents: Media Use and Attitudes Report'. Ofcom. https://www.ofcom.org.uk/__data/assets/pdf_file/0020/108182/children-parents-media-use-attitudes-2017.pdf.

Rideout, V. Roberts, D.F. Foehr, U.G. (2005), *Generation M: Media in the Lives of 8–18 Year Olds*. Menlo Park, CA: Kaiser Family Foundation

Rose, J. (2006), 'Independent review into the teaching of early reading'. DfES. www.standards.dfes.gov.uk/rosereview/report.pdf

Shield, B. and Dockerell, J. (2004), 'External and internal noise surveys of London primary schools'. *Journal of Acoustical Society of America*, 115(2), p.730–8.

Sigman, A (2012), 'Time for a View on Screen Time'. *Archives of Disease in Childhood*, 97, p. 935–942.

Appendix 1
Listening skills rating scale for Early Years

	Score	1	2	3	4
Looking at the person who is talking		Does not initiate eye contact simultaneously.	Some eye contact but not sustained.	Initiates eye contact but needs recall.	Appropriate eye contact when listening.
Staying quiet		Consistently interrupts/talks when adult is talking.	Occasionally quiet but cannot maintain this.	Some talking but can be recalled to stay quiet and listen.	Quiet when listening as part of a group.
Keeping still		Not able to stay on floor/mat. Constantly fidgets.	Inappropriate sitting posture/lots of fidgeting.	Stays on floor/mat but some fidgeting.	Appropriate balanced sitting.
Listening to all of the words		Does not respond to name. Does not respond to simple instructions.	Relies mostly on routine/copies others. Needs repeated reminders.	Follows very short instructions but needs repetition of more complex information.	Able to follow two-step instructions.
Total listening score					

Appendix 2
Group listening intervention – evaluation of progress

Names:	Looking at the person who is talking scores		Staying quiet scores		Keeping still scores		Listening to all of the words scores		Total listening scores:	
	Before	After	Before	After	Before	After	Before	After	Before	After
Totals:										

Appendix 3
Hello and Goodbye songs

Hello song

(to the tune of 'Frère Jacques')

Hello Jack, Hello Tom
How are you? How are you?
It's really good to see you!
It's really good to see you!
At listening time.
At listening time.

(Repeat for all children in the group)

Goodbye song

The clock says tick tock
The clock says tick tock
It's time to say goodbye
Goodbye Jack
Goodbye Tom
Goodbye everyone
It's time to say goodbye.

Appendix 4
Sample plan for small group listening work (3–4 years)

	Week 1	Week 2	Week 3	Week 4	Week 5	Week 6
Looking at the person who is talking	The 'Looking Song'	Who's got the glasses?	Round and round the hat goes	Find the space	Where's the bear?	Who is hiding?
Staying quiet	Sound boxes	Putting the toys to bed	Stop/go musical instruments	Loud and quiet musical instruments	Money Monster	Countdown
Sitting Still	Hopping frogs	'Dingle Dangle Scarecrow'	Traffic light waiting	Launchpad	Stop/go driving	Listen to what the Sergeant says
Listening to all of the words	Matching instruments	Listening for 'go'	Changing places	Old MacDonald's Farm	Who is hungry?	Sorting the washing

Appendix 5
Sample plan for whole-class listening work (4 years and beyond)

	Week 1	Week 2	Week 3	Week 4	Week 5	Week 6
Looking at the person who is talking	Round and round the hat goes	Where's the bear?	Who is hiding?	Who is cross?	Make the face	Who's got the crown?
Staying quiet	Sound boxes	Hunt the sound	Stop/go musical instruments	Money Monster	Don't wake the giant	Silent circle
Sitting Still	Hopping frogs	Wake up wand	Listen to what the Sergeant says	Animal run-around	Distraction bubbles	Statue tunnel
Listening to all of the words	Changing places	Old Macdonald's Farm	Actions to sounds	Who is hungry?	Farmyard swap	Seaside name story

Appendix 6
0–12 month development

Age:	Skill:	Why this helps listening:	How to help:
3-6 weeks	Making eye contact	Young children have single-channelled attention and need to look in order to listen. Encouraging eye contact helps them to focus on the person who is talking and also gives them lots of extra useful information that will help them to understand.	• Get down to your baby's eye level when talking to them. • Look at them when breast or bottle feeding them. • Avoid screen time for babies who are younger than 12 months old. • Choose a rear facing push chair or buggy so your baby can see your face.
1 month +	Showing a preference for voice over other noises	A speaker's voice need to be 15-20 decibels louder than the background noise in order for a child to focus on it. Reducing the background noise will help children to do this.	• Reduce background noise as much as possible. • Turn the television off when no-one is watching it. • Sing songs and nursery rhymes to your baby from birth.
6 months +	Turn taking with sounds	This is an important skill for conversation and teaches children that only one person talks at a time and the other person stays quiet so they can listen until it is their turn to talk.	• Reduce background noise as much as possible. • Look at your baby so they can pick up your non-verbal cues to help them take turns. • Copy the sounds they make to you.
6 months +	Responds to the emotion in parent's voice	This helps children to understand how people are feeling as tone of voice can change what people mean.	• Use lots of facial expression when talking to your baby. • Make sure your facial expression and tone of voice match.
12 months +	Turns to name	This helps children to recognise when people are talking to them and to listen to language directed at them. It is a useful skill to teach children to share attention with other people.	• Use your baby's name from birth. • Make up songs with their name. • Call their name and wait for them to look before speaking.

Appendix 7
Our listening work: information for parents

Listening is a special kind of attention – to listen we have to pay attention to sounds. Many children who have problems with listening are good with other kinds of attention. They may be able to sit and watch their favourite film for a long time or they may be able to concentrate for ages on their favourite toy. However, they may find it hard to:

- Listen to stories, especially in a group.
- Listen to you explaining something.
- Wait for their turn in a conversation or a game.

Listening is a really important skill for learning to talk but it is also a very important skill they will need at school. A good listener at school is more likely to understand what they have to do, remember new words and join in conversations with their new friends. In fact, if you're a good listener, you are more likely to be a good learner!

Just telling children to 'listen!' does not really help very much. This is because listening is quite a hard thing to do. It's not just one skill – it is several skills. In our approach to teaching children to listen, we aim to help the children learn the skills that make up good listening:

- **Looking** at the person who's talking.
- **Sitting still**
- **Staying quiet**
- **Listening** to all of the words

You can also help by reminding your child about these rules during the everyday things you do together that need them to listen. You can try:

- **Reminding them of the rule before you need them to listen:**

  Look at me – where are your shoes?

  I've got a surprise for you. When you're quiet, I'll tell you what it is.

- **Praising them when you can see them using the skills:**

  Well done, you kept really quiet and that helped you to do good listening.

  Brilliant! You listened right to the end!

- **Being specific about what they're doing wrong when they're not listening:**

  You're talking at the same time as me – that makes it very hard for you to do good listening.

This will really help them to use their new skills in real life.

Teaching Children to Listen in the Early Years © Liz Spooner and Jacqui Woodcock, 2019

Appendix 8
Games for parents to try at home

Looking games to try at home

Silent treasure hunt

What you need:

- Some 'treasure' to hide

What to do:

- Send your child out of the room and while they are gone, hide a box with 'treasure' in it somewhere in the room.

- Ask your child to come back into the room and find the treasure.

- The people in the room cannot tell the child where the treasure is but they can help them find the treasure by looking at where it is hidden.

Pass the turn

What you need:

- A game or activity that you can take turns in

What to do:

- Choose a game or activity which your child enjoys, e.g. a puzzle, a car ramp, a marble run or another game.

- Explain that you are going to give the people in the room a turn, but you are NOT going to say their name. You are going to look at them and give them a little nod.

- Then pass the turn to people one at a time by looking at them and nodding.

Staying quiet games to try at home

Musical traffic lights

What you need:

- An instrument such as bells or a shaker

- A stop/go sign

What to do:

- Encourage your child to play their instrument when they see the 'go' sign.

- When you turn the sign to 'stop', they must stop playing and try to keep their instrument quiet.

- You can then count to three before you turn the sign to 'go' again.

- Gradually try to count higher to see how long they can keep quiet.

Loud and quiet instruments

What you need:

- An instrument such as bells or a shaker

- Dino-loud and Mousie-quiet cue cards

What to do:

- Tell your child about Dino-loud (who likes loud noises) and Mousie-quiet (who likes everything to be quiet).

- Give your child an instrument.

- Put the Dino-loud and Mousie-quiet cue cards behind your back and bring one out to show your child.

- Encourage your child to play the instrument loudly when they see Dino-loud and then quietly when they see Mousie-quiet.

Sitting still games to try at home

Musical spots

What you need:

- Music

- Paper to make sitting spots

What to do:

- Try this activity in a small group with other family members.

- Put sheets of paper out in a circle, one for each person playing.

- Everyone walks or dances around the sitting spots while the music is playing.

- When the music stops, they can sit down on a spot, trying to keep still.

- Count to three before the music starts again and give praise for good keeping still.

- Try to very gradually increase the amount of time they have to sit still.

Traffic light waiting

What you need:

- Toy cars

- Stop/go signs

- Toy cones (or another object to mark start and finish points)

What to do:

- Set out the cones at either end of the room.

- Encourage your child to choose a car and try to keep it still at the start cone.

- They need to wait for you to turn the sign to 'go' and they can then push the car as fast as they can to the finish cone.

- Try to gradually increase the amount of time they have to wait before they can start their car.

Listening to all of the words games to try at home

Listening for 'go'

What you need:

- A suitable toy such as cars and car ramp or a marble run

What to do:

- Encourage your child to hold the car or the marble and wait for you to say 'ready … steady … go!'.

- You may need to help your child to begin with by putting your hand over theirs and gently encouraging them to wait.

- Try to gradually increase the amount of time your child waits before you say 'go'.

Listening for name

What you need:

- Bubbles

What to do:

- This is a good game to play with other family members.

- Blow the bubbles and then say someone's name.

- Only the person whose name was called can burst the bubbles.

- Remind your child to keep listening as you might call their name again.

Appendix 9
Choosing board

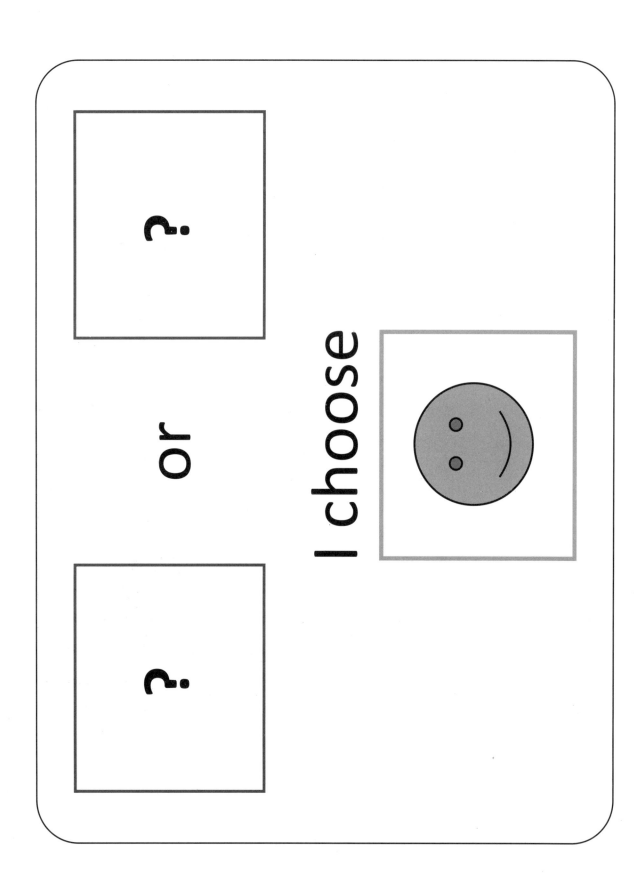

Appendix 10
Complex choosing board

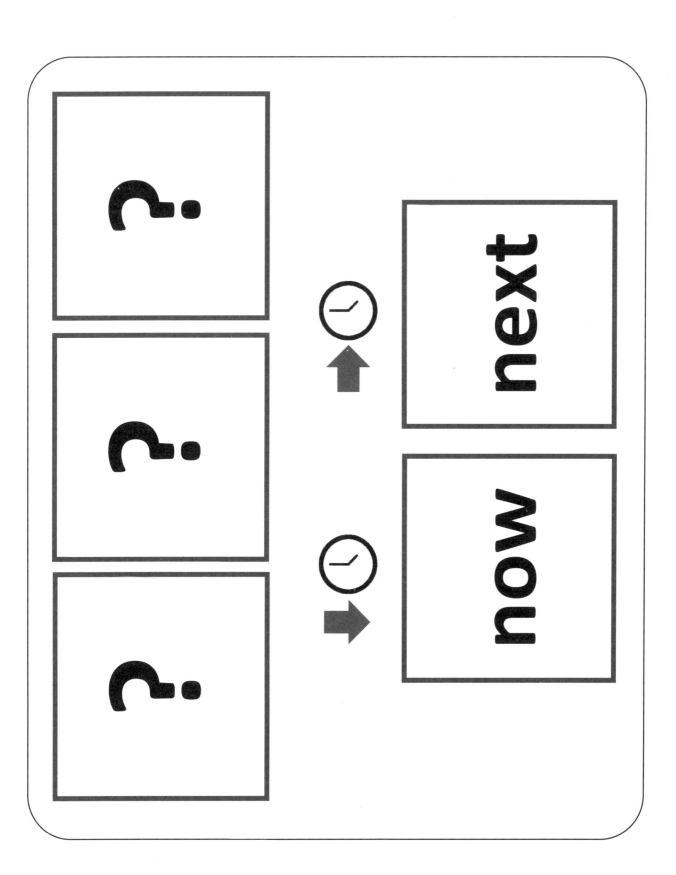

Appendix 11
Name story

Read the story to the children and insert different children's names into the story. When they hear their name, they must stand up and sit down. When you say 'EVERYONE', all the children have to stand up and sit down.

Going to the seaside

It was an exciting day. All the children in _____ were going on a trip to the seaside! The bus arrived and _____ got on first. Then _____ got on and sat right at the back. The journey was long. _____ fell asleep. _____ got very hungry and ate _____'s lunch and _____ sang songs very loudly all the way. When they arrived, _____ started building a sandcastle. _____ looked in the rock pools and _____ collected shells along the beach. Then it was time for lunch! EVERYONE got their sandwiches out. _____ finished their lunch first and ran down to the sea. _____ went for a paddle while _____ had a ride on the donkeys.

_____ finished their sandcastle and _____ helped them to get some water in their buckets. _____ found a crab under a stone and scared _____ with it.

Then it was time to get ice creams for EVERYONE. _____ had strawberry flavour. _____ had chocolate and _____ had vanilla with a flake. There was time for one racing game before they got back on the bus. _____ ran really fast but _____ won.

Then it was time to go home. _____ (name each child) climbed back on the bus and on the way home EVERYONE fell asleep. It had been a lovely day.

Illustration 1
Listening rules cue cards

Good listening is...

looking at the person who is talking

Good listening is...

staying quiet

Good listening is...

sitting still

Good listening is...

listening to all of the words

Illustration 2
Emotion cue cards

Illustration 3
Night-time and daytime cue cards

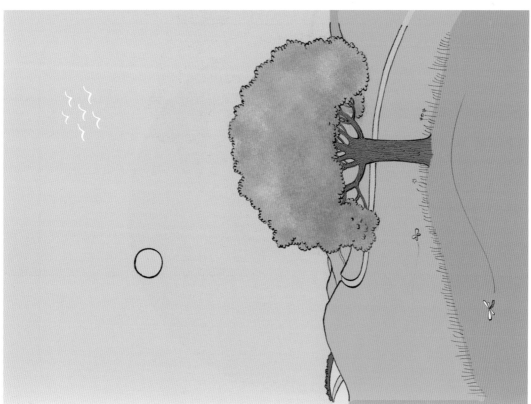

Illustration 4
Stop and go cue cards

Illustration 5
Dino-loud and Mousie-quiet cue cards

Illustration 6
Dino-loud and Mousie-quiet in rockets cue cards

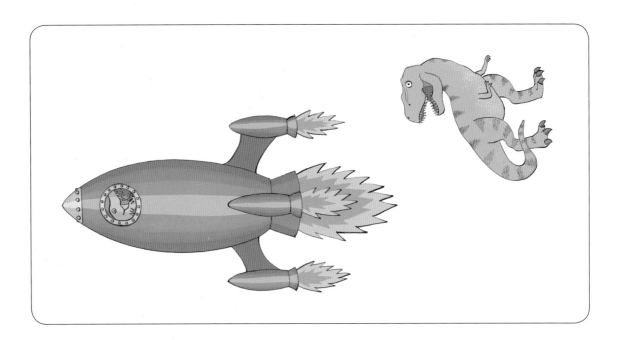

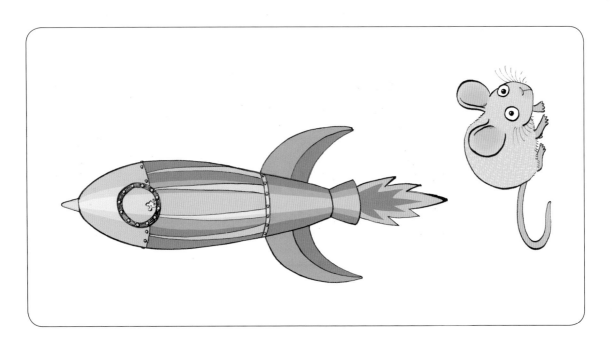

Illustration 7
Animal cue cards

Illustration 8
Animal food cue cards

Illustration 9
Letting your child lead poster

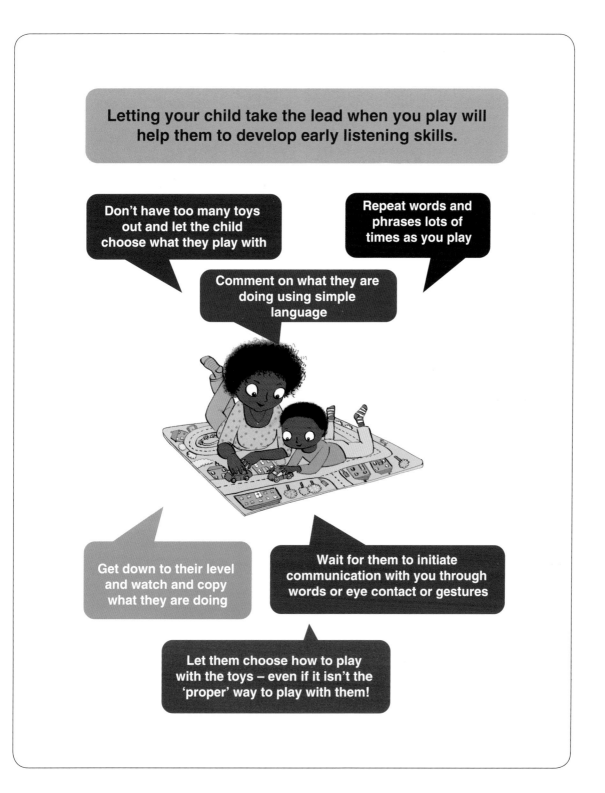

Illustration 10
Technology poster

Knowing the challenges and benefits of technology will help you give your child the best opportunities to learn to listen and to interact.

Join in! You can help them learn much more effectively by joining in with what they play. Look for interactive games that you can both play and talk about what you are watching together.

Be a good model. Children learn best through imitation so make sure you show them what you want them to do. When they talk to you make sure you look up from your phone or laptop so they know you are listening.

Manage screen time. Treat technology as you would any other environment a child spends time in. Adults should be in charge of how long children spend looking at a screen.

No-screen bedrooms. Tired children find it hard to listen and learn. You can help get a better night's sleep by making bedrooms a no-screen zone and making the last hour before bed time a time for listening to stories and talking rather than watching a screen.

Be aware of background noise. Noise from the television, radio or electronic games can really get in the way. If you are not watching it or listening to devices then turning them off will help make it a better environment for children to learn to listen.

Illustration 11
Listening fan

Listening to all of the words

Sitting still

Staying quiet

Looking at the person who is talking

Illustration 12
Crown cue card

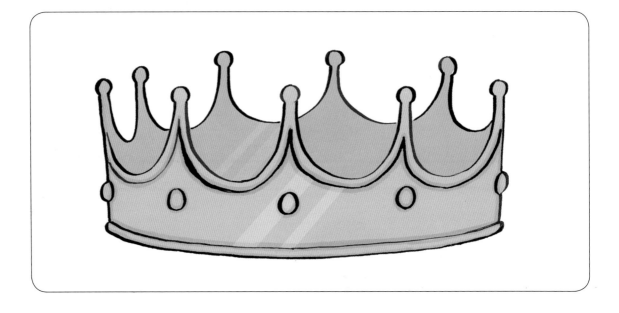